THE
WIN/WIN
WAY

THE
WIN/WIN
WAY

The New Approach

Transforming American

Business and Life

LUCY BEALE and RICK FIELDS

HARCOURT BRACE JOVANOVICH, PUBLISHERS

SAN DIEGO   NEW YORK   LONDON

Library of Congress Cataloging-in-Publication Data

Beale, Lucy.
    The win/win way.

    Bibliography: p.
    1. Success.   I. Fields, Rick.   II. Title.
BF637.S8B38   1987   158   87-11948
ISBN 0-15-197280-X

Designed by Janet S. Taggart
Printed in the United States of America
First edition
A B C D E

To my son Brian

L.B.

Contents

Acknowledgments

We wish to thank the many thousands of men and women who have participated in the Win/Win Business Forums, especially our colleagues in Denver and Boulder. They are committed to living the win/win way and have truly been a source of inspiration and encouragement.

John Penberthy, in particular, graciously shared his research on The Group, a Fort Collins real estate firm. Others include: Alec Tsoucatof, Sharon Huffman, Rod Yokooji, Barbara Bertin, and Martha Lawrence.

We also want to acknowledge the dozens of business people, executives and managers who shared their practical experience of the win/win way as well as the participants in Lucy's win/win presentations and sales seminars who have exchanged stories, presented challenges, and offered suggestions.

Finally, our deepest gratitude goes to our loved ones and our perfect teachers who have embarked with us on the win/win way.

Part One
CHOOSING
THE
WIN/WIN
WAY

1

The Case for Win/Win

IMAGINE FOR A moment that everything you do is a game. Imagine that your job is a game, or that your relationships are a game. Imagine that the most difficult tasks you have to accomplish are a game. Imagine that your life itself is a game.

When we think of a game, we naturally think of *winning* and *losing*. We may be playing against one other person, or we may be playing against a huge impersonal system—City Hall or some other bureaucracy. We may be playing against nature, or against a record—a time or distance or an amount of money—set by someone else. We may be playing against circumstances or against fate. We may even, knowingly or unknowingly, be playing against ourselves.

Imagine, then, that not only are we playing a game in everything we do, but that we are also *making up the rules* of the game ourselves. At first it might seem that every game must have a winner and a loser; but if we think about it a little more—as have the scientists involved in the complicated study of game theory—we might discover that the win/lose scenario is merely one possibility, a possibility which describes only one type of game. We can also imagine a game with a lose/lose scenario, strange as that might seem. With a little more thought, we can also imagine a game in which all the players could win, or in which one player wins by helping other players win as well. In game theory, this is called the win/win option. In this book we call it simply the win/win way.

People on the win/win way adopt an attitude—a way of playing, so to speak—producing interactions in which all parties—or all players—win.

The notion of everyone winning is not a new idea. In fact it has its roots in the Golden Rule: "Do unto others as you would have others do unto you." We might even say that the Golden Rule, which was first suggested almost two thousand years ago, is the guiding principle of the win/win game.

The goal of the win/win way is simple: that everyone involved wins. But its pursuit in the game of real life is often far from being simple or easy. At first, it might seem that learning to play a win/win game is one of the most difficult things you have ever tried to do. This is hardly surprising. For one thing, most of us have been brought up to believe that the win/lose game is the only game in town. Playing a win/win game—or living the win/win way— demands a whole new way of thinking. Yet the results are well worth the effort. The win/win game may be very chal- lenging; it is also very rewarding. In fact, if you learn to play the win/win game successfully, you will *always* win. After all, there are no losers in a win/win game.

On one level the win/win way is an attitude, a way of looking at the world and at yourself. Ultimately, it is your personal attitude that determines if a win/win transaction has been achieved. This means that if you lose, if you fail to find the key to a win/win solution, it is not appropriate to blame the other person. The rules of the win/win game don't allow blame. Blaming others is, as kids say when somebody doesn't play by the rules, "not fair."

You can create a win/win solution by yourself or with others. In either case, the win/win game will always involve everyone you come into contact with. At its highest level, the win/win game becomes the win/win way—a way of being, a way of life. It's also, as it happens, the most enjoyable and satisfying game there is. And any number can play.

What Does Winning Mean to You?

To play the win/win game successfully you first must decide what winning really means for you. This may not be as obvious a question as it might seem. For one person, winning might mean making a certain amount of money, or being invited to join an exclusive country club. For another person, winning might mean achieving personal freedom, or financial or emotional security.

Moreover, your definition of winning will probably change with every transaction. You might, for example, be able to define winning in a business deal in a relatively straightforward way—you want to make x amount of profit, for example. But you might also want to win in a way that leaves you with the possibility of continuing to do business with a particular person, especially if there is a chance that you might increase your profits in the future. In that case, winning would involve good will and good feelings on both sides. You might even decide that these things are more important for your success in the long run, and be willing to take less than you would have in the first place.

Many people think of winning simply in terms of getting more than they already have—or getting more than somebody else. An extreme, if humorous, example of this attitude is the slogan that appeared on T-shirts a few years ago: "Whoever dies with the most toys wins." There's certainly nothing wrong with wanting to acquire material possessions for your own enjoyment and pleasure, or with wanting to make as much money as possible—and the win/win way can certainly help you achieve these goals.

But that's hardly the whole story. Many people come to a point where they find themselves wondering if there isn't more to life than what they now have. At first it might seem that the "more" can be found in having more *things.* So they head for the stores or flip through the latest mail-order catalogues, and they acquire more stuff—only to find that once they have acquired a new pasta maker or a new life-size television screen they still don't have the "more" they were looking for.

Sometimes these people give up their search in frustration and disappointment, giving in to cynicism and bitterness. But sometimes—more and more often these days, it seems—they keep looking, until they find it in a place they hadn't even thought to look. That place can be found by discovering a new definition of winning. The most common definition of winning presupposes that for someone to win, someone else has to lose. It's either you or me.

The win/win way involves a shift in thinking, a redefinition of winning. Instead of you *or* me, it's now you *and* me. This means that instead of seeing the world as either win or lose, we realize that all of us could win. It means a change in keeping score. Instead of asking, "How much can I win?" the win/win player asks, "How much can I win with others?"

This mental shift is a subtle one. Subtle, yet very powerful in terms of personal rewards and public success. The shift from "you *or* me" to "you *and* me" can create major changes not only in our individual lives, but in the world as well.

Getting Out of the Win/Lose Box

In order for us to begin thinking in a new way, we first have to recognize the power of the hold that the old way of thinking has upon us. In order to think in the win/win way, we need to examine the reasons why the win/lose way has such a strong grip on us.

It's difficult to overstate the pervasive influence of win/lose thinking in our lives. And even then, recognition alone wouldn't help much to liberate us. "The competitive spirit is bred into us at an early age," observes Michael Korda in his best-selling book *Success!* "Ours is a society that requires and rewards a high level of competitive spirit, and values it far above cooperation and team-playing."

As children we learn the win/lose rules at an early age. Winners are rewarded in school and sports, and losers are made to feel that by not winning they have failed. Describing the results of a study of Anglo-American and Mexican-American students, Korda notes that "Mexican mothers tend to reinforce their children noncontingently, rewarding them whether they succeed or fail, whereas Anglo-American mothers tend to reinforce their children as a rigid function of the child's achievement."

It's not surprising, then, that by the time we have become teenagers, we've learned to accept the win/lose way of playing as completely natural—simply the way things are. Everybody wants to win, we've come to believe, and nobody wants to lose. "The whole world loves a winner," we're told, and we can see for ourselves how true this is. We can also see, if we care to, that nobody pays much attention to losers. By the time we have become adults, the win/lose way of counting life's successes and failures has come to seem so natural that hardly anyone ever questions it. Until recently, that is.

The bookstore racks and the library shelves are filled with books about this apparently basic human instinct. There are books on how to win at every possible activity—books on how to win in poker, blackjack, and roulette; books on how to win in business and in the corporate jungle; books on how to win at every sport; on how to win contests in newspapers and magazines; on how to win jobs in today's economy; and, of course, there are scores of books on how to win at love.

In nearly every case all these books about winning have one thing in common. They all assume that for someone to win, someone else has to lose. Even the books about winning a game of chance, such as roulette, emphasize the player's chances of "beating" the house.

Even the dictionary reinforces the idea that winning and losing are interdependent, rather like night and day. Webster's tells us that "win" comes from the Anglo-Saxon "winnan," which means "to strive, labor, fight, struggle." The cumulative effect of all these influences is that most of us assume that winning involves a battle with someone else—and that in order for one person to win, the other person must lose.

Some people relish this state of affairs. These are the people who buy books such as *Winning Through Intimidation* or *Looking Out For No. 1.* They see every interaction as a contest, a battle of wits, a war of strategy and nerves. Usually, people who see life this way win some of the time—or if they are very dedicated to winning, and if they study enough self-help books, they may even win most of the time.

But the law of averages, and the fact that there is always someone out there willing to stay up just a little later and get up just a little earlier, means that inevitably the roles will be switched one day. The winner will become the loser, and the loser will become the winner.

Of course it is possible, though not very likely, that someone will win all the time—or win many "big ones," whether they be football games or business deals—but even then there is almost always something lost. The "winner" wakes up one day surrounded by enemies—a by-product of having beaten everyone around. Or the "winner" may have neglected to develop genuine and meaningful relationships—spouse and family may have become virtual strangers. Winning, it seems, has suddenly lost its attraction—it has turned hollow and empty.

And thus we live on a perpetual seesaw of conquerer and victim, champion and loser, up one day and down the next.

The win/lose seesaw has evidently been in action for a long time.

"I don't meet the competition, I crush it," said Charles Revson, the founder of Revlon Cosmetics.

Cornelius Vanderbilt wrote, "You have undertaken to cheat me. I will not sue you, for the law takes too long. I will ruin you."

And this from Joseph Kennedy: "Don't get mad, get even."

The win/lose way may have worked in the past, but it is no longer effective in a world that gets more and more interdependent every day. Consider the following example:

Four years ago a certain computer operator for United Airlines was furious at her boss; she felt that she was losing. And so she set out to get even. She went up to the console of the main computer, hit a few keys, and left— having wiped out United Airlines' entire reservation system. It took two days and $1.5 million to get the system back on line.

This anecdote illustrates the havoc a single individual can cause in today's world. Similar incidents occur with some frequency, and are generally not even reported in the newspapers. According to the *Wall Street Journal*, industry now spends some $88 billion annually on drug abuse related problems. And what is drug abuse but the reflection of a win/lose relationship with oneself?

Win/lose thinking takes many forms. One of the most common is what is called "box thinking." In box thinking it's assumed that there are only two possible choices, or boxes. You are either in one box or the other. One of the most common boxes is the either/or box: "either I do what I love and I starve, or I do what I hate and earn a living."

Another common box is the attack/defend box. In this mind frame, you assume that if a conflict or contradiction arises, you must either attack or defend. Thus, any form of conflict or discussion about conflict is war—cold, hot, spoken, or unspoken.

Box thinking is win/lose thinking. Neither choice is the better way. As David Carradine, actor and star of the TV show "Kung Fu," says, "There is an alternative. There is a third way and it's not a combination of the first two ways. It is a different way." It is this same third way that Albert Einstein spoke of when he said that the atomic bomb had changed everything in the world except our way of thinking about it.

Finding the Win/Win Alternative

Finding the win/win alternative requires creativity and thought. It requires breaking out of ingrained habits of thinking, breaking out of the boxes of either/or and attack/defend. It may also require giving up assumptions about how things are, and how things have to be, or should be.

Finding the alternative doesn't mean "working hard," or trying to "make it work."

It doesn't involve struggle; it does require an atmosphere of calm, of cool thought. It's not working the angles; it's thinking *above* and beyond the angles.

It's not a matter of running after the alternative, but of sitting still long enough for the alternative to find you. It's being open to what some people call *intuition*.

It's not a matter of considering only what's best for me, or only what's best for others, but of considering what's the highest good for all concerned. If the solution is the best-for-all solution, then you have found the win/win alternative.

This alternative, of course, changes with each situation. There's an elusive quality to the win/win way because there's no one single answer. The alternative that's now easy and obvious is not necessarily the answer to the next situation.

Because of this changeable quality, it's not possible to make up rules about how to find the win/win alternative. Each situation is different, just as each individual is different. However, with practice, it *is* possible to master finding the win/win alternative in any situation.

It would be a mistake to think that the win/win way is just to be used situationally—that is, called upon only in certain situations. The win/win way is a whole way of life based upon the creation of harmony. To live the win/win way is to live on a very high level. After you have practiced it for some time, it will become visible in all the interactions you have, both with others and with yourself.

What the Win/Win Way Is Not

The win/win way is not altruism. It's not a matter of acting like a "nice guy" or a "goody-goody."

The win/win way is not about finishing last, or about compromise, or concession, or making do with less.

It's not about winning while people around you lose and grow to resent their loss—and you. (That resentment can come back to haunt you when you find your best efforts undermined and sabotaged by people waiting to "get even." Making people feel they have to get even with you is one sure way for all parties to lose—and the classic way to get yourself into a lose/lose situation.)

The win/win way is not about ignoring basic business common sense, such as having a good product, following a good marketing plan, using appropriate accounting systems, and building a well-trained sales force. It is important to know the critical success factors in your particular business, and how to use them. The win/win way doesn't excuse you from doing your business homework. If the functional parts of your business aren't in good working order, the win/win way will not help you.

The win/win way is not primarily about money and profits, though they often come about as by-products.

It is not possible to live the win/win way in one part of your life and not in every other part of your life. You can't live the win/win way at work and then go home to significant unresolved conflicts with your loved ones.

The win/win way is *not* manipulation of other people. Remember, the win/win way can be misrepresented. A salesperson who claims that if you were really a win/win person you would purchase this particular win/win vacuum cleaner, is not playing a genuine win/win game. Whenever a win/win approach is used to persuade you to accept someone else's self-interest as your own, it cannot be a win/win transaction by the very definition of the term. You must be free to choose what is best for you at all times.

The win/win way is not deal-making. It's not about saying, "You scratch my back and I'll scratch yours."

The win/win way is not unselfish. It is, rather, a truly enlightened self-interest.

The win/win way is *not* losing while letting others win. Whenever you feel you are losing, you are involved in a win/lose situation, just as much as when someone else feels that he is losing as a result of an interaction with you.

The win/win way is not trying to get even with someone, nor is it creating a situation in which someone wants to get even with you.

People resent it when you win at their expense. They will ultimately try to get even or get the better of you so that you lose.

Turning Win/Lose into Win/Win

Because the win/win way comes through transforming win/lose problems into win/win solutions, win/lose predicaments are actually "blessings in disguise." The sooner we recognize these predicaments and choose to appreciate them, the sooner we can turn them into win/win solutions. The hardest lessons in life prove to be the most fun—and the most educational—once we've sailed through them.

Most of us have been taught that our life should "work" all the time, and we feel guilty or discouraged when it doesn't. Yet we all have tough times, and difficult lessons to learn. Life isn't supposed to "work." It simply wasn't designed that way. Life was designed to challenge us. Remember, there are no solutions without problems. Things change constantly, and as you travel along the win/win path, you will constantly be presented with opportunities to create win/win solutions.

Every win/lose situation we encounter is a gift—the chance to create more winning in our lives.

If we see the world in win/lose terms—as most of us have been conditioned to do—we tend to attract win/lose situations. This is only natural. After all, we attract to us only that which we are: "Like attracts like," as the saying goes. This doesn't mean that the win/win way isn't working for us; it simply means we are attracting countless opportunities to create win/win solutions out of win/lose problems.

Every time you find a win/win solution, you will strengthen your win/win attitude, and you will attract more situations and events that are supportive of a win/win solution. As your win/win attitude is strengthened, you will draw others to you who also have a win/win attitude. If you sometimes have a win/win attitude and sometimes don't—which is how most of us are, especially in the beginning—you'll find that sometimes you attract people with a strong win/win attitude, and sometimes people who will create win/lose situations which you can transform into learning experiences—through which you can further strengthen your win/win understanding.

Guiding yourself through life the win/win way means that you encounter challenges as a person who wins and deserves to win, learning as much as possible in order to meet the next challenge. It means asking joyfully for the next lesson, so that you can create even more winning in your life.

People often complain that they would like to play a win/win game, but their boss doesn't and won't. Or it's the company's fault. People often say, "If only I could find a win/win company to work for . . ." or, "It's impossible to be a win/win person here because this is a win/lose company."

It may be necessary for you to get out of an environment which operates on a win/lose basis. Before taking this drastic step, though, take a closer look at your situation. Is it possible for you to begin by taking some small win/win steps—for example, with the people who work next to you? Most companies have a variety of situations in which win/win solutions work very well, and will be accepted by people who think of themselves as tough-minded win/lose types—if they can be shown that the solution works.

Before you say, "But then you mean it's up to me?"—the answer is "Of course, and you've always known it was, haven't you?"

A Better Way to Play

The win/win way is an idea whose time has come, an idea whose time is *now*. Lately the win/win idea is emerging as a way out of the impasse of win/lose thinking, not only in game theory, but in economics and business, international affairs and diplomacy. Not surprisingly, it has also received a great deal of attention from lawyers and others involved in the art and science of negotiation. The win/win idea is a new way of seeing how relationships of all kinds can be more fulfilling and satisfying. And finally, it is fast becoming a basic theme in many so-called self-help books—though the win/win way is really as much concerned with "other-help" (helping others, that is) as it is with self-help.

We live in a world where at last there are governments, political leaders, educators, business executives, and workers of all kinds seeking a better way. They are in search of better ways to increase productivity, govern fairly, end starvation, and educate our youth. In all these areas—and many others as well—the win/win path will be the playing field of the future. Those who do not choose to play on this field—in their relationships and in their businesses—may find themselves without a game to play.

2

The Business of Life and the Life of Business

ONE OF THE most exciting aspects of the win/win way is that it can be used with equal effectiveness in both your personal and your business life.

Most of us keep these two spheres in separate boxes— and winning in one all too often means losing in the other. Often we tend to see our personal life and our work life in win/lose terms. If we spend too much time and energy in one, we expect to lose in the other. People who are extremely dedicated to their work often allow their home life or their spiritual or artistic life to suffer, while people spending too much time on interests outside their office or workplace often find themselves overlooked or mistrusted when it comes time for promotions or increased responsibility.

From the win/win point of view, this way of thinking is needlessly limiting. If you have a problem in your personal life, it will reverberate in the workplace. And if your work is not satisfying, your family and friends will certainly know about it. People who follow the win/win way find that success in one sphere actually increases their success in the other. Winning in business can help you win in your personal life—and vice versa. According to the win/win way, your business life and your personal life—or *any* parts of your life for that matter—are not mutually opposed but are synergistic. That is, they work together; they co-exist.

This means that the proverbial whole is greater than the sum of the parts. When your personal life and business life support each other, the overall total quality of your life will increase in a way you never thought possible. Much of the power of the win/win way comes from the fact that it is basically always synergistic. Adding a win to a win almost always creates a new win that's greater than the mere addition of its parts. The opposite is also true, by the way. Win/lose thinking tends to create situations that end up as less than what you started with.

Our business and personal lives are not as separate as they might seem at first. In fact, both areas have one key element in common. In business, as in our personal lives, *relationships* matter more than anything else. According to the win/win way, relationships are the famous bottom line. If we create winning relationships, success will naturally follow in every area of our lives.

The Business of Business

A business cannot operate without people interacting with each other. These interactions create relationships, whether they last for years or for two minutes or two seconds.

A week without relationships would mean a week without meetings or phone calls. Initially this might sound appealing—but keep thinking. It would mean a week in which no letters were typed or received. No sales calls, no customer service, no conversations, no joking during coffee breaks. In short, no business transacted, no money earned. Simply put, no relationships means no business.

In order to manufacture or produce any product or service, say, a lawn mower, an extensive series of relationships must be established before the lawn mower can, in the final transaction, be purchased by a consumer. Someone must decide to produce the machinery, someone else must design it, and a whole team of technicians and workers must manufacture it. One person orders the necessary sub-components, someone else accounts for the order, and another person delivers it. People-relationships are involved in every step of the process, from management, to sales, to servicing.

The purpose of business, as everyone knows, is to make money, and this is accomplished through the relationships of the people at work. They, in turn, provide goods and services which other people either need or desire. This is true whether the buyer or user is another business, an individual, or a government. And these goods and services all support relationships at different levels. The ultimate purpose of every product or service is to serve people, thereby creating and nurturing specific relationships.

Take that lawn mower, for example. Its utility goes far beyond cutting grass. The person who buys the lawn mower uses it to keep the lawn from getting unruly, thereby enhancing the beauty of the home, in which the relationships of a family can take place. Even if the person lives alone, the lawn mower still in a way supports relationships with friends and neighbors who may visit, and even with the neighbors who may expect everyone on the street to do their part in keeping up the appearance of the neighborhood. Indeed, the lawn mower also supports the owner's relationship with him- or herself, in helping create an attractive appearance to the property.

Virtually every manufactured product in some way affects people in their relationships. An engineer or a theoretical scientist may work in relative isolation on an abstract project, but the final result will be a product that will ultimately serve human inter-relationships.

These relationships may be beneficial or harmful. Some relationships may result in the production of nuclear warheads; other relationships, in the establishment of families and friendships—in relationships of love. In any case, business is intrinsically designed to produce whatever consumers or buyers need in order to support their particular network of relationships.

Seen in this way, business takes on a somewhat different perspective. The critical importance of relationships in business is underlined by Alice Sargent's finding in *The Androgenous Manager*: Eighty-four percent of the people dismissed from their jobs are asked to leave because they cannot get along with their fellow workers, while only twelve percent are fired for technical or professional incompetence. People in business spend seventy percent of their time working with other people or in groups. Yet few of us have ever taken a course in high school or college that teaches us *how* to work with other people or in groups.

Management theories come and go—ranging from managing by objectives to managing by walking around—but all management theories recognize the need for people to foster good relationships in business. Seminars on how to create teams and how to get along with people are now becoming standard offerings in many corporations.

Good relationships are a critical factor in many businesses today, and they will be even more critical in the information society which is the wave of the future.

"During our agricultural period, the game was man against nature," writes John Naisbitt in *Megatrends*. "An industrial society pits man against fabricated nature. In an information society—for the first time in civilization—the game is people interacting with other people. This increases personal transactions geometrically, that is, all forms of interactive communication: telephone calls, checks written, memos, messages, letters, and more."

The conclusion is inevitable. Good relationships mean

good business. Better relationships mean better business. And bad relationships mean bad business.

From the Bottom Line

Bottom-line thinking that's fixated on profit and loss makes sense up to a point, but it is a very limited point. In fact, win/lose accounting is just that—the bottom line. Of course a business must make a reasonable profit to survive and continue to grow. That much, like good bookkeeping and accounting, is common sense.

But bottom-line thinking won't take us very far, and if it becomes the model for all our business planning, it can actually undermine our progress. It is largely because of such limited thinking that American business is in such trouble.

To begin with, bottom-line thinking is shortsighted. Long-range goals and plans are sacrificed for short-term profits. Managers stuck in win/lose thinking become stuck with producing a "win"—a profit, that is—each quarter. Regardless of the company's long-range interests, they're interested only in the immediate profit statements, which prove that they are "winners." The bottom line thus becomes a sort of scorecard in a competitive game.

This shortsightedness is often cited as one of the major factors in America's difficulty in competing with the Japanese, whose culture encourages short-term sacrifice for long-range goals. As Sony founder Akio Morita said in a recent *USA Today* interview, "The thing I don't understand is why Americans plan very short range." Win/lose and bottom-line thinking encourages short-range thinking.

Some win/lose business strategists take an even more drastic view. Instead of seeing business as a sort of competitive game, with winners and losers tallied up each quarter, they see it as an out-and-out war. If you believe that business is war, you find yourself attacking, defending, exploiting and—as such people like to say—taking no hostages. Planning sessions are run as war-game exercises against the enemy/competitors.

But if, as they say, war is hell, what does this make business? And if good relationships make good business, then what sort of relationships are created by viewing competitors and even others within your organization as the enemy? Viewing business as war may seem to work in the short run, but in the long run, it creates havoc and destruction on both sides. *Nobody* wins in a long, bitterly contested war. In fact, more often than not, a third party, who's been sitting out the conflict on the sidelines, comes in at a strategic moment to take advantage of the exhausted and depleted combatants. Wars may make victors for a time, but they also make losers, and they certainly make bad relationships.

To the Top Line

As we've said earlier, people everywhere are looking for a better way. People who have lost their jobs because of corporate mergers and takeovers, or because their companies couldn't compete with foreign firms, are all looking for a better way. People who work for companies that care only for the bottom line are looking for a better way. Managers are looking for a way out of the constant treadmill of ups and downs, wins and losses, vicious competition and endless pressure. People at all levels of business are saying, "There must be a better way."

The win/win approach *reverses* bottom-line thinking in order to find that better way so many people are looking for these days. According to the win/win way, parties negotiate not only for their own advantage, but for the highest good for all concerned as the end result of the deal. From a win/lose point of view, this is truly outrageous. It means sitting down and asking, "What's the highest good for our competition? What's the highest good for our employees? What's the highest good for our customers? For our accountants, for our bottom line? What's the highest good for the children of our country?"

We call this "top-line" thinking instead of bottom-line thinking. The top line is that place where the highest good of the greatest number of people concerned in any transaction converges. It is the win/win version of the bottom line.

Hidden Assets

When bottom-line assets within a business are measured only in dollars and cents, one crucial element is missing. As we have seen, business depends on relationships both inside and outside the organization. The *quality* of these relationships is thus an important part of any company's assets. But because relationships are intangibles—they can't be seen or touched or even systematically counted—people all too often forget how important they are to success in any endeavor. Good relationships are *hidden assets*. Unlike the visible assets of the bottom line, good relationships are hidden from view—way up on the top line.

Win/win relationships are top-line relationships, even though they may be hard to perceive at first. They are assets because without them good business is impossible. Good relationships also create that elusive asset called "goodwill," and sow the seeds of future success. When this is understood within a business, when good relationships are considered an asset, fully as much as profits or fast-moving inventory, action can be taken to create success on every level. This includes increased profitability, greater employee retention and reduced turnover, higher fair market share, as well as real contributions to community and society.

Of course, business relationships are the sum total of

countless interactions between individuals. The internal assets of a company ought to include the sum total of what we might call the *inner* assets of the people working within the company. These inner assets include how individuals feel about themselves, and the amount of satisfaction and fulfillment they find in working for that company. The way people feel about themselves is a clear reflection of the *quality* of the relationship with self.

People who feel encouraged to promote win/win relationships in the workplace find their jobs inherently satisfying. They are thus more likely to keep working enthusiastically even if business is in a slump, or if they run into a particularly difficult challenge. The feelings of satisfaction that people find in themselves and in their relationships with others when they live and work according to the win/win way comprise one of a company's most valuable assets, even if they can't be displayed on the bottom line in terms of dollars and cents.

The internal assets of an organization are the same as the internal assets of the individual expanded and multiplied. A corporation's assets have meaning only if they reflect a company's ability to be successful in business. That ability, when we look up from the quarterly bottom line, is nothing other than the ability of people in the company to interact in ways that result in win/win results for everyone concerned.

The feelings of satisfaction people find within themselves are hidden assets, too, which do not show up on the "bottom line." We each have a relationship with our own life, and it's the most important relationship we have—for without that, how could we have a successful relationship with anyone else? But this self-relationship is not an obvious one, for it exists within ourselves, and is, in the deepest sense, immeasurable.

In business, as in life, relationships are the key. Our hidden assets are also our most valuable ones.

3

Competition, Cooperation, and the American Way

IS LIFE A zero-sum game? Is it a game, that is, in which you lose what I win, or I win what you lose—a transaction in which one player's loss is literally the other player's gain?

If we look at the way contemporary American society is structured—the way we bring up our children, run our schools, conduct our business and work, and even the way we play—the answer would have to be "yes."

Zero-sum games are based upon a strict win/lose model, which is to say that they are based upon *competition*. When you play a zero-sum game you play by competing with the other person. The other person, of course, becomes your opponent.

We live in an intensely competitive society; we have all grown up learning to compete. In fact, most of us believe that competition is itself the "American Way of Life." In a recent study of the larger issue of competition, *No Contest*, journalist Alfie Kohn gathered evidence from hundreds of sources showing how pervasive competition is in our lives.

"Our economic system is predicated on competition," writes Kohn, "while our schooling, from the earliest grades, trains us not only to triumph over others but to regard them as obstacles to our own success. Our leisure time is filled with highly structured games in which one individual or team must defeat another. Even within the family there is rivalry—a muted but often desperate struggle that treats approval as a scarce commodity and turns love into a trophy.

"Thus it is," concludes Kohn, "that Vince Lombardi's famous comment—'Winning isn't everything; it's the only thing'—must be understood not merely as the expression of one football coach's fanaticism, but as a capsule description of our entire culture. Our lives are not merely affected by, but structured upon, the need to be 'better than.' We seem to have reached a point where doing our jobs, educating our children, and even relaxing on the weekends, have to take place in the context of a struggle where some must lose . . ."

According to Kohn's research, there are two major types of competition.

The first is called "structural competition." Structural competition is external. It depends upon "the win/lose framework." Its primary characteristic is "mutually exclusive goal attainment." This means, says Kohn, that "my success requires your failure. Our fates are negatively linked . . . two or more individuals are trying to achieve a goal that cannot be achieved by all of them." This, of course, is the very essence of a zero-sum game like poker.

The second type of competition may be thought of as the psychological result of structural competition. This is what Kohn calls "intentional competition." Intentional competition "is internal," says Kohn. "It concerns the desire on the part of the individual to be number one." We are all familiar with people whose lives exhibit a high degree of this sort of psychological competition—for example, the man who walks into a party bent upon "proving" that he is stronger, smarter, or cleverer than anyone else who is there.

The Way Things Are

Not surprisingly, most of us have come to believe that we must live our lives competitively because "this is just the way things are." But this is not really so. Living in a constant state of competition only makes sense if the "way things are" means that everything in our personal and business lives really *is* a zero-sum game.

As we've discussed, most of us tend to think of all games as zero-sum games. This is because the games we have been raised on, and the games we continue to watch (if not play) in our adult years are zero-sum games—games in which one side loses while the other side wins. They are, in short, the sort of games that a competitive society would be expected to favor, both as a reflection of its existing structure and as a means of training people to act in a competitive way, thereby perpetuating that structure.

The only hitch to this theory—and it is a big hitch—is that life is *not* a zero-sum game. Nor, as it turns out, are most businesses.

The Way Things Really Are

Our lives are not, as we've just said (but it's worth repeating) zero-sum games. Our lives are not, that is to say, games in which one person loses what the other gains. Our lives are not, to use Alfie Kohn's term, structurally competitive. Nor, for that matter, are they psychological competitions. You don't win the game-that-is-your-life by beating other people, nor do you win the game-that-is-your-life by always having to be better than other people. You win the game-that-is-your-life by being yourself. That's the key.

Nor is most business—contrary to much popular and "expert" belief—a zero-sum game. Zero-sum games are games in which "counters" are moved from one player to another. Zero-sum games don't create new value, they merely transfer already existing or invented value (as in poker, where the chips may stand for already existing money or merely for themselves) from one player to the other. Nearly all business, however, creates or adds value to the world. That "added value," after all, is what a business markets.

Zero-sum business games, on the other hand, include such things as highway robbery (in which your gain is my loss), or, at a higher level, the kinds of financial speculation and takeovers that increasingly are being recognized as harmful to the economy as a whole.

"Healthy" Competition

But surely, you're probably thinking at this point, there is such a thing as *healthy* competition, as opposed to excessive competition. Competition builds character, creates excellence, makes life fun, and gets things done.

This, of course, is what we've all been taught. But let's look a little closer.

First of all, does competition *really* create excellence? Travelers who fly today's airlines, with the drastic decrease in service and quality resulting from fierce competition and government deregulation, would say no. As would viewers of highly competitive American television, which compares so unfavorably to the non-competitive BBC. Competition, it seems, can often affect excellence adversely—especially when companies pay more attention to ratings or profit than to quality.

Competition can be harmful to excellence, also, because it encourages us to pay more attention to our competitors than to our customers. It's all too easy to blame "the competition" when you lose a sale or lose market share. But while "the competition" is the most readily available scapegoat, it almost always makes more sense to look carefully at your own business for the answer. Perhaps your product or service isn't meeting the customer's need. Or perhaps you didn't do the best job possible marketing, presenting, and selling your product.

In either case, it is you and your product, not the competition, that's preventing your success. And it's you and your product, not the competition, that holds the key to your success as well. Excellence isn't created by paying excessively close attention to what "the other guy" is doing.

Many organizations have learned the hard way just how destructive competition can be. In 1986, for example, the Denver Chamber of Commerce tried to utilize competition as a way to get new members. They organized their volunteer salespeople into teams, and pitted the teams against each other. As the battle for "the best" team heated up, the competition got rough. There was considerable backbiting, and bad feelings were rampant. Some people even seemed more interested in seeing the other team lose than in seeing their own team win.

By the end of the year, it was obvious that the program was a disaster. The recruiting teams had actually brought in fewer new members than ever before. Of the fifty volunteers, only six had signed up for the next year. Usually, almost half of the volunteers each year were veterans.

The following year's results were also low. But this time the management held training sessions, and encouraged the volunteers to work for the benefit of both themselves and the community. Win/lose competition, it was clear, had created only losers.

Competition and Relationships

The problem with competition on a personal level is that it pits one person against another. And in doing so it can pit you against your own best interest. Competition, therefore, can erode not only your relationship with another person, but also with yourself.

A person who competes wants to be better *than*, to have more *than*, and to be superior *to*, another person. This obsession with comparing yourself with another person is, psychologists tell us, the result of a lack of self-worth or self-esteem. Being insecure or unsure of who we are, we attempt to prove our value and worth by constantly comparing ourselves with others.

Of course, it doesn't work. In fact, if you try to build up your self-esteem by competing with others, you're only covering up your real problem. You're not giving yourself the chance to discover the source of your true self-worth. How can you, when you're constantly worrying about comparing yourself with everybody else? Comparison and self-judgment, coupled with a low sense of self-worth, combine to create a driving need to compete and to prove oneself better than other people. When you feel that you have to beat other people, it is, sad to say, because you yourself feel beaten.

We all have different qualities and strengths. Often it makes no sense at all to compare these different qualities and strengths—in fact, it's like comparing apples and oranges, or apples and horses! People who have a sense of their basic worth, people who know who they are, or who are enjoying finding out who they are, don't need to make others feel bad in order to make themselves feel good. They value their own special skills and talents, and they value the skills and talents of others as well.

Competing as a way to build self-esteem can sabotage our best efforts in many subtle ways. Let's listen for a moment to Joe and his girlfriend as they discuss Joe's business prospects over dinner in an elegant restaurant. Joe is a well-groomed, successful-looking man in his mid-thirties. He has recently spent over a year putting all of his time, money, and energy into an extremely high-risk business venture. Not unexpectedly, and due to no fault of Joe's, the venture failed.

Now Joe needs a job, hopefully one with an income that will allow him to maintain his comfortable life-style. He is also, not unnaturally, feeling a bit insecure. But Joe would never admit that he's not feeling on top of the world—not to himself, not to his friends, and certainly not to his girlfriend.

What he does tell her goes something like this. He's describing his chances in the job market. "You know I'm terrific at what I do," he says, as the drinks are served. "I'm better than ninety-five percent of the guys in the business." By the time the appetizers are brought to their table, Joe is telling her how his business would have made it, and "blown everybody else clear out of the water," if only he'd been able to run things his way. During the main course, he says: "There are hundreds of companies that would be begging for me to work with them, if they knew I was available."

By the time dessert and coffee arrive, however, a new note has crept into Joe's voice. His girlfriend, as you probably guessed, has hardly said a word since they sat down. "Now tell me," Joe is demanding, "aren't I right? Isn't it true?"

By the end of his monologue—and by the end of the meal—Joe is no longer pointing out how much better he is than everyone else. He's seeking reassurance and agreement that he is indeed, as he's said earlier, "a super guy." Both of these verbal tacks come from the same place—his own feelings of fear and inferiority. Feeling superior and feeling inferior are two sides of the same coin. Sometimes it's heads (you're better), sometimes it's tails (they're better). But you will never get the answer you need. That can only come from yourself.

Competition Addiction

Some people feel that they couldn't possibly live—or work—without competition. They feel that competition adds "spice" to their lives, that without the thrill and excitement of the winners and losers game, they wouldn't be motivated to do anything. They're like the people who say they can't get out of the house without something to pick them up and get them going—that "something" may be coffee and cigarettes or alcohol or even drugs.

No doubt competition can create a certain amount of excitement in life and work. There's an undeniable "rush" or high that comes from the suspense and the adrenaline generated during a battle—and the high can be even higher when and if you win. (And the crash, as with other drugs, can be just as severe.)

The problem is that there's no *end* to competition. It takes more and more "winning" over other people in order to help you to feel good about yourself. When your primary frame of reference for success and well-being is how you're doing on the competitive battlefield, a little is never enough. There's a psychological dependence upon competition as a way to stay motivated and to keep on achieving. People who are addicted to competition are lost when they can't locate more people/opponents to compete with. They've never discovered their *own* passions and motivations. The other person is always the yardstick.

Win/Win Competition

Is it possible to utilize competition in a win/win way—to compete in a win/win game? Win/win competition *is* possible, though it is very different from the win/lose competition we're all so familiar with. In fact, win/win competition may not seem like competition at all, and many people might even say that there's no such thing. But let's think for a moment about what it might be, *if* it does indeed exist.

In win/win competition you want to win *and* you want others to win as well. You want to be the best that you can be, and you want others to be the best that *they* can be.

In win/win competition, you compete with yourself. You

strive to improve your own performance, to add value to yourself and to others—as well as to express yourself more fully and creatively in your life as a whole. But you're not "competing with yourself" in a frenetic and frantic search for self-fulfillment—an aggressive and unbalanced search that might be unproductive or even harmful. Rather, you "compete with yourself" in a loving and balanced way so that you create harmony within yourself and within your life.

In win/win competition, you learn from others so that you can utilize the marketplace as an information source. You learn more from your customers than from your competitors. You ask your customers what they want and need. And you do your best to provide it. You examine the marketplace to see what it needs. You use your time and energy to create and produce the best products and services you can—without spending all your time worrying about what the "competition" is doing.

IBM is a good example of a company that encourages win/win competition.

IBM salespeople are trained to speak about their competitors with respect. In any sales presentation comparing an IBM product with a competitor's product, the material must be very carefully prepared to show how well the IBM equipment will meet the customer's needs—and not what is wrong with the competitor's equipment. In fact, IBM's policy manual states that any salesperson who disparages the competition will be summarily dismissed. And they hold to it.

Finally, win/win competition is fun. It's fun because it is an expression of your passion about life and of your personal freedom. In win/win competition you're not limited by what others can or cannot do, but only by what you can imagine yourself doing. You are free because you're not constantly measuring yourself against others. You are genuinely your own person; you're an individual who isn't concerned with being better *than*. Your sense of confidence and self-worth isn't determined by others; nor is your uncertainty or hesitation—which we all naturally experience now and then—masked by the need to present yourself as a great competitor. Your self-esteem is genuine, and comes from your sense of who you are and how you contribute to yourself and others.

4

Playing the Win/Win Game

IF LIFE IS not a zero-sum sort of win/lose game, and if competition can actually do more harm than good, we must next ask ourselves what sort of game life actually is—and what kind of interaction could possibly replace that of competition.

This is not an easy question. Our society is so deeply structured along win/lose lines that most of us have a hard time imagining a *game* without winners and losers—let alone a whole way of life or a complete society without them.

Anthropologists such as Margaret Mead have studied a variety of different cultures, and have discovered that some societies, like ours, are extremely competitive, whereas others are less so, and still others are more cooperative than competitive. Some people might object that the most highly cooperative societies Mead studied—such as the American Indian or Polynesian societies—are so different from our own that they cannot teach us much. But we can at least learn from these societies that competition is not, as is often claimed, inevitable or the result of "human nature." Co-operative societies are real possibilities.

Recently social scientists have utilized game theory in studying the issue of competition and cooperation as it appears in what they call a non zero-sum game. In a non zero-sum game, as we shall see, the point of the game is to increase value rather than to move points from one player to another. An example of a non zero-sum volleyball game, for example, might involve counting the number of times the ball is successfully hit back and forth over the net without touching the ground. In non zero-sum, in other words, competition between players is replaced by cooperation.

Game theorists have studied non zero-sum games with intriguing results. One particular game is called "Prisoner's Dilemma." In its simplest form, Prisoner's Dilemma involves two players. At each turn, they may choose to either cooperate or defect. Neither player knows what the other will do, just as two prisoners kept in two different cells would have no way of knowing if their partner was "cooperating" or "defecting."

If both players cooperate, they each receive three points.

If both players defect, they each receive one point.

If one player cooperates and the other player defects, then the player who defects receives five points, and the player who cooperates receives zero. This last situation is called the "sucker's payoff," and obviously presents a temptation to defect.

From the point of view of either player, it seems to make sense to defect at each play. By doing so, you'd receive either five points (if your partner cooperated) or at least one point if your partner defected.

But suppose your partner thought the same way you did. Then he would also choose to defect each time, and you would both end up with only one point per play. The final score would be considerably higher if you both decided to cooperate, thus receiving three points at each play.

Prisoner's Dilemma, then, presents us with a paradox. If each player pursues a logical course of self-interest, both players will end up with less than if each had pursued a course of cooperation. But, of course, neither can be certain what the other will do.

"The Prisoner's Dilemma is simply an abstract formulation of some very common and interesting situations," says political scientist Robert Axelrod in *The Evolution of Cooperation*, "in which what is best for each person individually leads to mutual defection, whereas everyone would have been better off with mutual cooperation."

One version of Prisoner's Dilemma that's been popular in many business schools and business seminars is called "Win As Much As You Can." The game is played in groups of eight which are divided into two-person partnerships. The game is played for ten rounds; the fifth and eighth rounds are "bonus rounds" in which both the losses and wins are multiplied by three for the fifth round, and by five for the eighth round. In the tenth and last round, the bonus value is increased ten times. The partnerships are not allowed to discuss their choices with other members of their group until round five, and then once again in round eight.

Often the game begins with many people playing defect. But by the fifth round, when all the partnerships within a group can discuss the game, someone usually points out that if everyone plays Y (cooperate), then everyone in the group will score as high as possible.

But there's almost always somebody else—some "wise guy"—who will then vote X (defect), reasoning that if everybody else votes Y, the defecter will do better than everyone else. The bonuses in the fifth and eighth round, of course, increase the temptation to defect.

Fred E. Jandt, author of *Win-Win Negotiating*, has played this game with groups drawn from the conflict-management seminars he has given for companies and organizations such as McDonnell Douglas, Datapoint, Disneyland, Weyerhauser, Xerox, and the U.S. Department of Labor, as well as for firms in many other countries throughout the world.

"The quintessentially cooperative players have faith in each other from the start," he writes. "They look at the system of scoring and recognize that the group will benefit most if each player selects a Y in each round. It never occurs to these players that someone else in the group may choose an X to the other players' Ys and thereby upset the group's apple cart—or if it does occur to them, they trust the others not to do it.

"Competitive players, meanwhile, are innately cynical and seek any advantage they can get. They not only try to outguess their group-mates; they may even, during rounds when discussion is permitted, lie about what letter they intend to choose."

Dr. Jandt found also that players from the United States, as well as players from France, Italy, and Germany, had "a decided tendency toward competitive play." In Japan, on the other hand, he finally stopped playing the game altogether because everybody there cooperated as a matter of course. "The members subordinate individual goals to the desire for the group's success against other groups, trusting that their own personal success will be a result of the group's success."

Jandt draws three conclusions from his seminar experiences with "Win As Much As You Can":

1. Don't assume that everyone else shares your goals.

2. Whether or not others share your goals, your success or failure depends upon how *they* play as well as upon how *you* play.

3. Whether you win or lose, you can learn a lot by watching the other players. In fact, the biggest value of the exercise is that it gives you insights into how you and others play in the biggest game of all, *life*.

Tit for Tat

Is there a winning strategy for the Prisoner's Dilemma/Win As Much As You Can game? To find out, Robert Axelrod asked game theorists, political and social scientists, computer scientists, psychologists, economists, and mathematicians from all over the country to submit computer programs to play in a Prisoner's Dilemma computer tournament.

The first round had fifteen entries. The winner was a program submitted by Anatol Rapoport, a psychology professor. The name of this program was "Tit for Tat," and it was the simplest and most straightforward of all the programs. As Axelrod says in *The Evolution of Cooperation*, "Tit for Tat is the policy of cooperating on the first move and then doing whatever the other player did on the previous move. This policy means that Tit for Tat will defect once after each defection of the other player."

The Tit for Tat strategy did so well that Professor Axelrod decided to give all the players another chance. He sent them all the program scores, along with details about Tit for Tat. This time there were sixty-four contestants. And once again, Tit for Tat came out on top.

A Winning Win/Win Strategy?

Is there a general strategy that will help you find the win/win solution in a variety of situations? Of course, it's difficult to generalize, since every situation is obviously different, but the overwhelming success of Tit for Tat in the Prisoner's Dilemma tournament gives us some valuable guidelines for finding the win/win solution to any problem.

To begin with, the win/win solution, the solution that does the best for all players, is itself based upon cooperation and not upon competition. And the Tit for Tat program begins by cooperating. It does so because it knows that the game it's playing is not a zero-sum game. "The interests of the players are not in total conflict," as Axelrod points out. "Both players can do well by getting the reward for mutual cooperation, or both can do poorly by getting the punishment for mutual defection. Using the assumption that the other player will always make the move you fear most (which is natural in competitive zero-sum games) will lead you to expect that the other will never cooperate, which in turn will lead you to defect, causing unending punishment."

This first move is called a "nice" rule or strategy—"which is to say never being the first to defect." As it turns out, the highest-scoring players in the tournament had this rule in common. So we could say that the first lesson to be learned from the Prisoner's Dilemma tournament is that it pays to be nice—at least in non zero-sum games.

Tit for Tat is reciprocal: it answers a defection with a defection. This approach is important for players who want to develop a win/win strategy, because all too often people think that win/win means you lose and the other person wins. Win/win means *both* players win. Playing a win/win game doesn't mean giving in.

Tit for Tat is "forgiving." As soon as its partner realized that unending reciprocal defections would result in a downhill spiral, and made a cooperative move, Tit for Tat would forgive and go right back to cooperation. "Tit for Tat is unforgiving for one rule," explains Axelrod, "but thereafter is totally forgiving of that defection. After one punishment, it lets bygones be bygones."

Tit for Tat is a very clear and open strategy. After just a few moves, every other player knew exactly what it was going to do. Tit for Tat had no tricks or surprises. Most of us think of a skillful strategist as someone who is either holding something back, or as someone who knows what the strategy is, but keeps it hidden. This may be true in win/lose competition, but it is apparently not true in a non zero-sum game where cooperation is rewarded. There it pays to be open, straightforward, and clear. There are no wild cards in Tit for Tat.

Another important strategic consideration is that the

Prisoner's Dilemma was played over a long stretch of time. The longer the play went on, the more important cooperation became. If the game were played for only one round, the temptation to defect would mean that the player who defected had a fifty/fifty chance of winning five points or one point. The disastrous consequences of playing "defect" only show up in "the shadow of the future," as Axelrod calls it.

The implications of "the shadow of the future" for a win/win game player are clear. In business and in life, play as much as possible with people you intend to keep playing with for some time. Get-rich-quick schemes in business (as well as one-night stands in relationships) probably will not bode well for playing a win/win game.

Though, as we said, there is no one strategy for playing a win/win game, the suggestions drawn from Professor Rapoport's Tit for Tat are well worth keeping in mind—especially since they take into account the fact that we are trying to play a win/win game with others who are playing with a win/lose set of mind.

Here, then, is Professor Axelrod's summation of why Tit for Tat was such a winning win/win strategy:

"What accounts for Tit for Tat's robust success is its combination of being nice, retaliatory, forgiving, and clear. Its niceness prevents it from getting into unnecessary trouble. Its retaliation discourages the other side from persisting whenever defection is tried. Its forgiveness helps restore mutual cooperation. And its clarity makes it intelligible to the other player, thereby eliciting long-term cooperation."

In other words, a win/win strategist begins with generosity, responds with accuracy, doesn't hold grudges, keeps everything out in the open, and finally, keeps on playing.

Part Two
SETTING
YOURSELF
UP TO WIN

5

First, Take Care of Yourself

THE FIRST STEP on the win/win path is learning how to set yourself up to win.

This first step is essential. If it's overlooked, if you begin by trying to create a winning situation for others before you've created one for yourself, the chances are that you will stumble and fall. You can lose and lose badly.

In order to set yourself up to win, you must first acknowledge and accept your current reality. You must tell yourself the truth about the way your life is. This reality is always your starting point. It's the foundation of your current situation; it is where you stand. And in order to successfully play the win/win way, you must have your feet planted squarely on that ground.

You're in a very powerful position when you know and acknowledge exactly where you are right now. It is not as easy to do this as it might seem. The basic point is that you must look at your life objectively, at least to begin with. Making judgments about what is good and bad, worthwhile and not worthwhile, interesting and tedious, can actually be a way of hiding from ourselves. Instead of seeing what is really going on, we see only our subjective ideas and opinions—our thoughts, fears and hopes—about what is happening.

Being honest about the "cold hard facts" of your current situation is important. Take some time out, by yourself, to look at your life. Give yourself this interlude; treat yourself to some time alone—sitting quietly by yourself in a favorite park, taking a walk on the beach, or listening to music.

Which relationships are joyous and satisfying, and which are not? What exactly is the current reality of your work situation? Do you enjoy it? Are you satisfied? What would you change?

Ask and answer such questions as these without judgment, without concern for what's "good" and what's "bad." Try not to view your life either positively or negatively. *Just view it.*

An important part of setting yourself up to win is learning how to take care of yourself. Taking care of yourself *doesn't* mean beating the opposition. It means *caring* for yourself. And that means making friends with yourself. And *that* means getting to know who you are. This takes time and attention, especially when life is as crowded and busy as it is for most of us.

Next, Take Care of Business

The next step in setting yourself up to win is to take care of business. It's important to ground yourself firmly in the reality of the business world.

To prosper in business, you must hire efficient and trustworthy employees. You must establish adequate accounting systems. You must know the market.

In every job and every business, there are many other factors critical to success. These are unique to each industry. For example, one of the keys to success in the wholesale distribution business is to keep your inventory turnover high, meanwhile keeping your inventory levels as low as possible.

A major part of your job is to learn about the "critical success factors" in your field. Read as much about the industry as you can; study books and trade publications. Talk to other professionals who "know the ropes." They might seem reluctant at first to share their trade secrets with you, a potential competitor. But, in fact, people love to talk shop. If you are truly interested in what people have to tell you, you will assuredly find someone interested in talking to you.

Just as there are critical success factors particular to each industry, there are similar components to be found in each position within each company. For example, some managers expect their subordinates to be strong "team players," whereas others favor strong individual performances. One secretarial position may require top-notch word-processing skills; in another, it may be more important to keep the boss on schedule. It's important in setting yourself up to win that you be as clear as possible about what the pivotal factors for success in your position and industry are.

Ultimately, one of the best ways to learn is by making mistakes, acknowledging them in a reasonable and intelligent manner, and then following up with the necessary corrections. Nothing inhibits success as much as the fear of failure, which is really the fear of making mistakes. But from a win/win point of view, one person's mistake is another person's opportunity to learn something new. Knowing how to transform the loss from a "mistake" into the "win" of a learning experience is crucial to discovering the critical success factors in any business.

Barriers to Setting Yourself Up to Win

One of the most surprising discoveries people make on their way to the win/win path is that no matter how much they may *think* they want to win, there is some part of them that feels more comfortable losing. It's more often *you* that makes you lose than someone or something outside yourself. In order to play the win/win game with others, you must first be able to play the win/win game with yourself.

People engage in self-sabotage by playing against themselves on a variety of different levels. Sometimes people allow themselves to win on one level—getting a raise, for example—only to sabotage themselves by turning down a challenging promotion. Or they allow themselves to win in business, but not in personal relationships. Allowing yourself to win at one level is no guarantee that you will allow yourself to win at another level.

There are many psychological explanations of the "fear of winning." Often it can be traced back to early childhood conditioning. Little girls may fear that they will lose their parents' love if they do better than their brothers; or children might somehow be given the message that they will get more attention and concern when they fail. Some psychologists trace the fear of winning back to the child's fear of competing with a parent. Others point out that many people are afraid to win because they feel that winning provokes the envy—and the anger—of others. But no matter where this fear comes from, it's important to realize that it is present, to some degree, in all of us.

This sort of "programming" can be obvious or subtle. But wherever it comes from, the challenge is to recognize it when it comes into play, and then to go on to make winning choices. If winning creates too much anxiety in you, try observing your feelings and thoughts during small wins at first, and then go on to bigger things. Because your fear of winning is basically just programming—unconscious messages you have accepted as true—you can simply reprogram yourself. And adopting the win/win attitude is one of the most powerful tools available for you to change your unconscious programming.

The barriers that can prevent you from setting yourself up to win can take many forms. Here are eight of the major barriers to watch for on the win/win way.

1 The Victim Barrier

Some people enjoy playing the role of the victim. For them, creating a win/win way of life means having to give up the security and self-righteousness of the victim's role. Victims always blame everyone or everything other than themselves—the other person in a relationship or business deal, or the circumstances, or the environment, or the weather. Victims never take responsibility for their actions. Victims are never to blame. This is what we might call the victim's revenge.

Most people stuck on the victim barrier would never admit it. They insist that they are "innocent" victims. And in their conscious minds, they are.

From a certain point of view, people who proclaim that it's not their fault that they're victims are correct. There are many ways in which our society actually encourages people to feel victimized. Many of us have been encouraged to play the victim because as children we received lots of attention when we were sick, or when we got the worst of a fight at school.

For example, it's commonly assumed that germs and bacteria cause illness—in other words, we are their victims. Yet how can we explain the fact that some people catch a germ-borne illness while others do not? Why is it that some people experience miraculous recoveries from serious illnesses while others do not? And how is it that some people manage to live free of any disease?

The answer partly depends upon the degree to which we perceive ourselves as victims, and this springs from the various types of conditioning we've been exposed to all our lives.

Our inner programming is very powerful, but there are

ways in which we can free ourselves. Whenever you find yourself losing, try to uncover the "losing tapes" that you carry deep inside you. Just notice if you can find that place, or if you can hear that voice. We all have "weak spots," and we are all vulnerable to them.

Once these inner tapes are recognized, you'll be amazed at how quickly they lose their power. One executive in a major computer firm confided some thoughts he had during a business meeting. He was on the losing side of a conflict when he heard his internal voice telling him that he was not good enough to win. He then silently asked that voice: "Where did you come from?"

The voice replied, "From when you were six years old and your older brother wouldn't let you play baseball with him and his friends. And again, when you were a teenager and the other kids laughed at you because your haircut looked so funny."

Another businessman, a real-estate developer, remarked that he had somehow concluded that he couldn't be really successful because he was short. He had made himself a *victim of being short.*

We all make ourselves victims of something or other. It is well worth the effort for you to discover your reason, or reasons, for not wanting to win.

Once you truly want to win, you will begin to become aware, one by one, of all the barriers to winning that are hidden inside you. And this is the first step toward conquering them.

2   The "I Don't Deserve to Win" Barrier

This barrier tells you that you don't deserve to have what you want, that you're not worthy or good enough to win. One woman tells this story:

"I once believed that I did not deserve to be thin. At that time being a thin person was the most important and significant thing I wanted. As a result, I stayed fat. As long as there was a strong message inside me that told me that

I didn't deserve to be thin, that I was not good enough to be thin, I remained an overweight person.

"When I realized that I was sabotaging my efforts by the 'not deserving' programming, I began to tell myself over and over again that I deserved to be thin. Once I believed I deserved it, and corrected the 'non-deserving' programming, I became thin quite quickly."

You cannot live the win/win way if you believe that you don't deserve the things you want. You *must* believe that you deserve to win. And you must believe that others deserve to win as well.

3   The "I Can't Win" Barrier

The "I can't" barrier results from feeling powerless and helpless. How many times a day do you find yourself saying "I can't" to yourself?

"I can't" is very powerful, but it is *hardly ever true*. How many stories have you read about people who fight City Hall and win? Or about people who are faced with enormous and debilitating physical or emotional handicaps, and win?

"I can't" is rarely true. What *is* almost always true is "I won't." Now *this* is very good news. Because you can change "I won't" to "I will" in an instant. "I will" doesn't demand great strength or intellectual power. It requires only the willingness to try.

As the president of a chain of retail clothing stores tells his staff, "Can't doesn't."

4   The "You Don't Deserve to Win" Barrier

You cannot set yourself up to win unless you want *others* to win—all others, with no exceptions. No doubt this is a big order, one which will probably seem impossible at first. But we can all take a step in this direction by sincerely wishing others well. A Buddhist exercise designed to develop our capacity for goodwill advises us to practice in small steps. Begin with yourself, then go on to family members and friends, and then extend your good wishes to acquaintances and people you feel "neutral" about. Finally, see if you can include people who have annoyed you, and then go on to include people you may be angry with. Eventually, you should be able to include everyone in the world—"all sentient beings," as the Buddhists say—all of creation.

Don't worry at first about whether you can actively encourage others to win. Just go step by step. The important thing is to be moving in the right direction—the win/win direction.

Most of us realize that our actions affect things in the physical world—for example, when we flip a switch, the corresponding light goes on. It is possible that this same principle, the law of cause and effect, is just as true in the world of thought. Perhaps you've noticed that revenge ultimately does not work, that it's not productive to say or dwell on unkind thoughts. It is quite likely that when you live to beat someone else, someone else will beat you—sooner or later.

5   The "What Others Say" Barrier

The next barrier to setting yourself up to win is that of listening to everything others say—and believing it. In some cases, societal expectations can be a serious barrier to your winning. For example, until quite recently, women were not expected to be successful in the business world. Another example is the familiar belief that serious artists must necessarily live in poverty. Or that "real" men dominate others.

Early childhood conditioning includes the beliefs your parents and teachers and siblings gave you about yourself. These beliefs often include subtle messages about your ability to win—or even about the desirability of winning. You may have been told in school, directly or indirectly, that you were not as smart or capable as other children. You may have been told that it was wrong to win, or that you should let others win. You may even have felt that your parents did not want you to win.

It's important to keep in mind that what others say about you is *always* and *only* their perception of you. Listen carefully to every piece of feedback and information that you get—and then decide whether you want to accept it or not. Do this with family, friends, co-workers, bosses and employees, casual acquaintances and even strangers in the street. Maintain this same critical stance when you listen to the news or read a newspaper. Learn to trust your own perceptions and feelings. You can't set yourself up to win if your definition of winning is based upon what others say and do.

If someone tells you that you shouldn't set yourself up to win, question that also. Don't let anyone take away your right to win.

6 The Positive-and-Negative Thinking Barrier

Thoughts are very powerful things. Nearly everything we use in our daily lives began as a thought, a plan, an idea. When you think of yourself as being a winner in a win/win world, chances are that's just what you will be. And when you think of yourself as a loser, chances are *that's* what you will be.

It might seem obvious, given the above, that positive thinking will produce positive results, and that negative thinking will produce negative results. At first glance it *does* seem quite straightforward. But from the win/win point of view, things are not always so simple.

According to the win/lose way, positive thinking is defined as positive *when it is contrasted with negative thinking.* But we must take it a step further. Ultimately, the win/win way *transcends* both positive and negative thinking. In fact, identifying positive thoughts as "good" and negative thoughts as "bad" can block your progress on the win/win way.

To begin with, positive and negative are not absolutes.

What one person perceives as positive can be perceived as negative by another. From the win/win perspective, thoughts are *just thoughts*. They may be "good" in one situation and "bad" in another. They may be productive in one situation, and less than fruitful in another. It's only when you learn to free yourself from both positive and negative thinking that you're in a position to use *all* your thoughts as steps on the win/win way.

Both positive thoughts and negative thoughts are a part of the natural movement of the mind. Similarly, both positive experiences and negative experiences are part of our lives. The win/win way does not guarantee that you will have only positive thoughts, nor does it guarantee that only things that you like will happen to you. But it does show you how to master both positive and negative experiences so that you will have the ability to recognize every thought and action as an opportunity to create a win/win life of harmony and fulfillment.

Negative thoughts are not inherently "bad;" they become a problem only when we let ourselves get stuck in them. But although negative thinking can certainly erode our self-confidence or our ability to win, it can also clue us in as to how we're really feeling and help us to become more aware of our emotions.

We can use negative thinking to help us turn a difficult situation around, thereby creating a win/win situation. Negative thinking is valuable; it must simply be utilized effectively. Don't ignore negative thoughts; they're eloquent indications of earlier programming—which can be rewritten. Use them to initiate productive action.

7 The Down-Cycle Barrier

We all go through various phases or life transitions, such as leaving for college, getting married, getting divorced, experiencing illness, changing jobs, or moving to another city, to name just a few. It is at these times in particular that we may become lethargic and depressed.

Annie Denver, the ex-wife of the songwriter and singer John Denver, tells of a time when she was very unhappy. She was sleeping more and drinking a bit too much at cocktail parties. Now, seven years later, she observes that this period of unhappiness served her well. It led her to question her values, which were causing her pain; it helped guide her to personal freedom, happiness and joy.

As we move through difficult transitions, we have the opportunity to turn depression, lethargy, boredom, and anxiety into joy and happiness. In other words, such transitions can be the catalysts for growth.

People must grow. Most of us do it only when we have to, for it is often painful. Moving toward the win/win way more likely than not is precipitated by a major life crisis or a series of small ones.

When you are confronted by a crisis, large or small, it is crucial to see it as the next important step on your way to the win/win life. Greet the hard times as eagerly as you greet the good times. People experience cycles just as business does. The challenge is to live the tough times with as much joy and vigor as you live the good times. And that is possible when you live the win/win way.

8 The Lack of Self-Love Barrier

Taking care of yourself is, as we have seen, the first and most basic step in setting yourself up to win. Having a high sense of self-esteem or self-love is the advanced version of that first step. People with a sense of self-love not only take care of themselves, they also enjoy and delight in their lives. They allow themselves to win in such a way that other people are drawn to them—and find that they win, too.

When we truly love ourselves, we naturally take care of ourselves. We nurture ourselves. We look out for our own well-being. We avoid putting ourselves in situations where we will get hurt. We eat only the foods which contribute to our health and well-being, and avoid substances which can be harmful, which for many people include alcohol, sugar, coffee, chocolate, cigarettes, and drugs—including over-the-counter and prescription drugs, as well as the illicit ones.

When we truly love ourselves, we make sure that the cars we drive are safe and well-tuned. We give ourselves enough rest; we take adequate time for play and relaxation as well as for meaningful work. We surround ourselves with people who support us, and who want us to win.

When we truly love ourselves, we create an environment for ourselves that expresses our self-love. Our homes are safe, aesthetically pleasing, and calming. The home becomes a refuge, a place where we can recharge and restore ourselves. This doesn't require lots of money or elaborate interior decorating schemes. It requires only care, attention, and imagination.

The same is true for clothing. It's not necessary to worry about "dressing for success," but it does make sense to realize that what we wear sends signals to both other people and to ourselves. When you truly care about yourself, your clothing will reflect that. It will be clean and appropriate. Your shoes will be polished.

This "environmental care" will contribute more than you might think toward your ability to set yourself up to win. Your environment is made up of lots of little details, which may not seem very important—but they are. For one thing, precisely because your environment is made up of many small components, it's easy to work with and change. You may not be able to set yourself up to win all at once, but you can certainly start by taking care of some small detail— putting your clothes in order, cleaning or decorating your home, starting that exercise program by taking a long walk. And don't forget—all these details, when taken together, add up to something big. They are the pattern, the design, of your whole life.

It *is* easy to let things slip when you are busy or tired— or when you get too involved in "winning" in the old win/lose way. Or when you get depressed, or when you are in an arduous transitional period of your life. It's especially easy to let things slip when you're in a "down cycle." But it's just at those times that it is most important to take care of yourself first, and to treat yourself with loving attention.

Having a high sense of self-worth is important in setting yourself up to win in relationships, too. It is necessary to love yourself first before you can accept love from others. If you're unable to accept your own love, how can you accept another person's? When you try to accept love from someone else before you accept it from yourself, you're putting yourself in a position of dependency and need. And when that happens, you're setting yourself up to lose. But when you truly love yourself, your life reflects that, and you will attract people who can share and enjoy that love with you. Then setting yourself up to win will become a way to set others up to win, too.

Knowing. Doing. Being.

In working with the material in this chapter—in working with your own life, that is—it is important to keep in mind the differences between *knowing, doing,* and *being.* Books can only instill *knowing.* This knowledge can then be incorporated into what you already know. But knowledge can take you only so far. Then it's up to you to move *knowing* into the day-to-day activities of your life. This is the realm of *doing,* where knowing takes on flesh and blood and bones. It is only in *doing* that knowing becomes real. And it is only by *doing* that knowledge becomes your own.

The state of *being* is much more difficult to describe, although we all have experienced it at some point in our lives. In the state of *being* there is no effort. It's like breathing: we're usually not consciously aware of our breathing, and yet it's absolutely critical to our life, every single second. It *is* our life. It's natural and spontaneous and joyous.

It is in this state of *being* that we truly live the win/win way. We are then in harmony with the flow of life—in which everything that happens is for the good of all that is. As you practice the *thinking* and *doing* of the win/win way you will, perhaps, begin to notice that you spend moments, whole minutes, then even hours and days in a place of *being*—and harmony—with all creation.

Then you will know that you have set yourself up to win all your life.

This is the secret of the win/win way. You must go through the ups and downs of learning how to set yourself up to win. But as you practice the win/win way more and more, you will have more and more moments of effortless, joyous being.

You will realize that the win/win way is your birthright. It is your natural state. In fact, it's impossible to lose once you are in a win/win state of being. Being on the win/win way means that you *always* win. After you have learned to set yourself up to win, you will realize that it was all a joke—a big joke, a cosmic joke, you might say. Then you will know that you have been set up to win from the very beginning.

6

Passion

THERE ARE THREE golden keys to the win/win way—we call them the keys of *passion, time,* and *team.*

Passion is the first key. We might even call it the master key, the one that unlocks the doors to *time* and *team.*

Passion is the master key because it's the key that opens you to your *self.* It's the key to the enjoyment of life and work. You cannot win if you do not work your passion.

When you're doing something that is your passion you are already winning, no matter what the outcome. Finding and expressing your passion is an indication of the high quality of your relationship with yourself. The expression of your passion in the world will ultimately affect many other people, of course, but the responsibility for finding and expressing that passion is yours alone.

Your passion is yours and no one else's. No one else can give it to you, nor can anyone take it away from you. Whatever people might say—whether they approve or disapprove—it neither enhances nor detracts from your passion.

Furthermore, no one can tell you what your passion is.

They can tell you only what they observe about you and your interests, but no one else in the world has exactly your passion in life. Your passion is *uniquely* yours. It is your mission. This means that your expression of it is valuable to the world. If everyone in the world expressed their passion fully, then the world would most certainly be a better place to live.

Work for Something Money Can't Buy

Working just to make a living doesn't ultimately make much sense. When you work just to make a living, it means that you put in forty hours every week so that you can have a good time on weekends. It means that most of your waking life is spent on an activity that is, perhaps, boring, frustrating, and unfulfilling.

When your work and your passion are the same—or at least related in some way—the above situation is reversed. Then you are working for far more than money. You are working for something money can't buy—you are working for your own pleasure and enjoyment. You are working for your own passion. When you work for your passion you are working for yourself, and you cannot lose. You enjoy your work. You take pleasure in what you make or produce or sell or buy. You take pleasure in what you do. You're not one of those people who are always phoning in sick so they can take the day off. You're not the victim of stress or burnout or of quiet desperation.

Everybody has a passion in life, though not everybody knows what it is. It can be anything, though. To Sarah, for example, it's something as simple and ordinary as selling. Sarah went to work for IBM right out of college, selling in their Information Products Division. She was a fantastic salesperson.

Then she left IBM when her children were born. But in the hectic years of caring for two small children, she still found time for her passion: she sold benefit tickets for the symphony and worked on numerous fund-raisers for volunteer organizations. She sold stationery to raise money for a not-for-profit corporation. As Sarah says, "Just give me something to sell, and I'll sell it."

When her children were old enough to not require her full-time attention, she took a part-time job selling professional-women's clothing. And she became a "super sales star" there as well.

Sarah is a person who doesn't stop selling. She loves it, and she does it whether she is paid for it or not. She is rewarded by the *process* of selling. She takes pleasure in the challenge, in the communication with the other person, in the intelligence it takes to match a buyer with a product, the back-and-forth play of negotiations. Sarah sells for herself first, and then for others. Of course in doing this, she also benefits the people she sells to as well as their friends and families.

People like Sarah, who work for something that money cannot buy, work for love and joy and fulfillment. They work to make a difference in their own lives and in the lives of others. Though the "something" money can't buy is intangible, it contributes to such tangible rewards as good health and well-being. When people concentrate on working for that intangible "something" they often end up with the tangible reward of money. Money seems to come naturally, as a by-product, to people whose work is their passion. It might be just enough to support them, or it might be much more—but when your work is your passion it doesn't matter all that much. You already have your reward.

People whose work is their passion don't separate work and leisure the way most people do. It's said that Steven Spielberg, the movie director and producer who brought *E.T.* to the screen, shoots home movies on his vacations. A venture capitalist in Hollywood takes extravagant vacations each year, charting a barge to tour the vineyards of France or engaging a yacht for a leisurely cruise of the Greek

Isles. But he always invites associates who are involved in one or another of his business ventures to join him. It could be said that he takes his passion with him—literally.

Or consider Stephen Jobs, the founder of Apple Computers. At the age of thirty-one, Jobs can do anything he wants to do. He can go anyplace in the world. His wealth is estimated at around $150 million. But he chooses to remain in Silicon Valley, where he started Apple Computers, putting together another computer company. This time he wants to do for educational computers what Apple did for personal computers.

"When he left Apple there was no adventure he could not have tried . . ." begins an article in a recent issue of *Esquire* focusing on "Americans at Work." The article continues: "Yet he wound up forming a company in which he is re-creating as closely as possible the life he knew before: the life of not just work but nonstop work, no-other-life work. Why is this the path he chose?"

The answer is that Jobs is passionate about his work. "My self-identity does not revolve around being a businessman, though I recognize that is what I do," Jobs told the *Esquire* reporter. "I think of myself more as a person who builds neat things. I like building neat things. I like making tools that are useful to people. I like working with very bright people. I like interacting in the world of ideas, though somehow those ideas have to be tied to some physical reality. One of the things I like the most is dropping a new idea on a bunch of incredibly smart and talented people and then letting them work it out themselves. I like all of that very, very much."

Finding Your Passion

An executive at Control Data Corporation in Minneapolis says that the luckiest people in the world are the people whose life is their work.

How can you become one of these people? To begin, you have to discover, rediscover, or verify your passion. This may take some doing, especially if your passion is covered over by years and years of working only to earn a living—or if you've been living just to get by and please others. But your passion *is* there, hidden somewhere deep within you, and finding it is an exciting and important adventure.

First, make a list of things you cannot resist doing—the things you do no matter what else is going on in your life. You might list a sport, a hobby, anything you do for your own enjoyment and pleasure. It might be a certain kind of work—such as working with computers. Or it might simply be a characteristic you display in relationships and friendships. You might, for example, say: "I am always the center of attention," or "I always end up the accountant or the manager." One woman says, "I am the person who always ends up organizing the filing cabinet and procedures in the office."

Then list all the things you did as a child and as a teenager which made you feel happy and successful. Maybe you were in 4-H, or maybe you rode ponies or designed clothing or organized games.

Now list what does *not* work for you at all—whether it's being a manager or selling or answering the phone all day. Maybe you hate small talk, or working alone—or working with other people, for that matter. The important thing is to be as specific as possible about what turns you off.

By now you may feel as if you have written a small book. But there is still one final list to make—your "wildest dream" list. Suppose time, money, age, health, gender, and education weren't considerations. What would you do? Be thorough. Be spontaneous. Record every thought, every possibility, no matter how small or seemingly ridiculous.

Use Your List

Now sit and spend time with your lists. Study them. Look for patterns. Remember that *you* know who you are better than anyone else.

Notice the patterns. Your passion may change form, but it is bound to recur from time to time. The essence of your passion will be revealed by the underlying pattern in the things you love to do.

Get started on your wildest dreams. You may have written, "Be a ballerina and dance on the New York stage." And that might seem like a crazy idea, if you're forty years old, say, and living on a sheep farm in Wyoming. Yet why not enroll in a dance class and see where it leads? You may not make the big time, but taking that first step may lead to something you just can't imagine right now. You might be led to *another* dream or to a career that you would never have thought of pursuing. Only by taking that first step can you discover the passion that is the key to making your life an adventure.

One woman's wildest dream was to be a wardrobe consultant. She went right out, found a partner who was already in the business, and got business cards printed. It took her two months to discover that the work was not as glamorous as she had imagined. Cleaning out other people's closets did not appeal to her for long.

She closed up the business, having managed to break even financially. She then moved on to her *next* wildest dream, which was to sponsor and coordinate a business conference. This time, the work was everything she had hoped it would be, and now she runs a successful agency setting up business conferences and seminars across the country.

Once you know what your passion is, allow yourself to *do something about it.* Send for information, read a book, take a class or seminar. Buy a paintbrush, if you want to be a painter. Remember, no step is too small—as long as it is eventually followed by another step, and then another.

Your Own Backyard

Sometimes you will find your passion in what you are already doing. You might just have to take off the blinders that you have put on from years of habit.

Take John, for example. John is a butcher in the San Francisco Bay area. After working in a large supermarket for twenty years or so, he felt increasingly frustrated, anxious, and disappointed. He quit and gave himself six months to find his passion. He was searching—for a way to make a contribution to others and to make a difference in the world. In those six months, he read books about working; he attended seminars and workshops. He consulted job counselors. At the end of the six months, he felt that he had found his passion.

He returned to the supermarket and went back to cutting meat, but this time it was with a difference. He had discovered that his passion had never been cutting meat. His passion was the interactions he had with other people. He figured that he could have these interactions no matter what he did, so he chose to continue cutting meat.

He began to have more meaningful conversations with the other butchers behind the window. When the buzzer rang indicating that a customer wanted a special cut of meat, John was quick to respond.

He worked with each customer differently than he had in the past years. He began to get to know them as people. He was on a first-name basis with many of his customers; he knew about their families. He was always happy to discuss the best cuts and how to cook them.

Within a few months, customers were lining up at the butcher window to have John cut their meat. He had transformed an entire department and perhaps an entire supermarket—because he was living his passion.

Three Words You Can Forget When You Find Your Passion

Commitment

The first word is *commitment*. Commitment is necessary when you're not sure of what you are doing or of who you are. A person whose work is his passion doesn't "need to be" committed because he already *is* committed. Commitment is a natural characteristic of passion. Can you imagine Einstein wondering if he was committed to physics or the theory of relativity?

Some marketing and sales jobs put a great deal of emphasis on commitment. Barbara was at first enthusiastic about her new job as a representative of a line of fine china. She had gone to Chicago to attend a marketing job-fair. The speakers pressed the audience for commitment, whipping the would-be sales representatives up into a veritable frenzy of excitement. Barbara got caught up in the emotional atmosphere and eagerly signed up.

When she returned home she started working at her new job, but without the support of the pep talks and constant encouragement, she found it difficult to "keep her commitment." When she made a list of her wildest dreams, she realized that neither sales nor china appeared anywhere on her list.

She had gotten into the work because *other* people loved it, had shared their enthusiasm with her, and had convinced her that *this* was what she wanted. But it wasn't what she wanted. It wasn't *hers*. She had not yet discovered her passion—and so she was vulnerable to somebody else's idea of what her commitment should be. When she discovered that her commitment wasn't a lasting one, however, she was then able to embark on the great adventure of finding out what her passion really was.

Working at relationships or making relationships work amounts to the same thing. Either they have an innate passion and harmony, or they do not. Certainly the harmony and passion require nurturing and development, but they need first of all to be there. When you are at one with your passion, then you will be naturally and spontaneously committed. If you ignore your passion, or if you accept someone else's passion as your own, then you will find yourself struggling to create commitment to no avail.

Competition

The next word you can do without when your work and passion are combined is *competition.*

People whose work is their passion don't see "beating the competition" as proof of winning. They simply do the best they can at whatever they do. They rely upon their creativity and the expression of their passion to do a job well.

If you use competition with others as a way to motivate yourself, you might try asking yourself how you would perform if there *were no competition.* Would you still be doing what you are doing? If the answer is no, you have still not put your passion and work together.

People who work their passion don't care what the competition is doing. The yardstick for their own performance is not how well someone else is doing. They do know and understand the marketplace, and they are aware of what others in the same field are producing. But they don't *measure* themselves against others. In fact, if you base what you do on what the competition is doing, you will probably find your performance going down. Measuring your performance against someone else's will throw you off track; it will actually impose limits on your own potential.

Remember, every person is unique and has unique talents, skills, and contributions to make. It is essential that you express your own uniqueness—and that you help people around you express theirs. When you understand that no one else can make *your* contribution, you'll realize that competition simply doesn't make sense.

Motivation

The last word you can do without when your work and passion are joined is *motivation*. You don't "need to be" motivated in order to do work you love.

If you feel that you lack motivation, it's probably because you are not doing work that expresses your passion. Most people in this situation look for motivation from other people. This external motivation can take the form of talks with your boss or your co-workers. You might also read motivational self-help books, take motivational seminars, or listen to tapes in your car or as you jog. In any case, you can be sure that you are not the only one out there who feels the need for external motivation. Motivational speakers and motivational products are big business these days.

True, this form of motivation can work for a while, but the drawback is that it must be continually reinforced. It can even become addictive. You need more and more in order to be productive. The biggest problem with external motivation, of course, is that it requires someone or something outside yourself to do it for you. You're not relying upon yourself. And when you rely upon a source outside yourself, you can just as easily be de-motivated. What someone else says or does can cause you to feel rejected, incompetent, and discouraged. You can feel this way only when you rely upon what others say and do to give you a sense of your own well-being.

If you rely upon external motivation, it may be difficult for you to find your passion and live it. If your motivation comes from someone who for their own interest wants you to do a certain form of work, it may be hard to leave—even if that work does not allow you to be true to your passion.

Only you know what your passion is. Other people can

make recommendations and share their observations with you, but they cannot tell you what it is. If you rely upon outside approval, you run the risk of never finding your passion.

Think about the times you have done your best at anything. Was it because of someone else, or was it because you did it as an expression of yourself? Chances are that you gave your best when you were doing what you loved, regardless of whether someone approved or disapproved.

Celebrating Wins

Internal motivation is much more reliable than external motivation. When *you* motivate yourself you're relying upon yourself and no one else. It's much easier to find your passion then, and to live it.

The best way to build internal motivation is by celebrating "wins." A "win" is anything you've accomplished, anything that you've done or that has happened to you which you consider to be a win. A simple exercise that helps you celebrate wins is this: all you have to do is keep a spiral notebook and pen next to your bed. Every night before you go to sleep, record ten wins you had that day. Record all the obvious wins first: closed the big sale, received a promotion, was given a beautiful present, gave a beautiful present.

It would be very unusual for you to have ten *big* wins in a single day, however—especially at first. So after you have recorded the big wins, go on to the small, perhaps seemingly insignificant events that let you see yourself as a winner. These wins can be very simple—things like practicing patience with your child in a trying situation, or eating a healthy breakfast, or attending an exercise class. Some people even record *writing their wins* as a win!

Even a mistake can be rewritten into a win. You might, for example, write something like this: "I really blew it today. I did _____. What I learned was _____ and I don't need to do that one again." That certainly would be a win!

Record your wins this way every night, and then "sleep on it." Doing this exercise every night before bed for a year will establish you firmly in internal motivation. It takes about a year because it takes that long to reprogram your subconscious—which has been formed by the way you've lived and the thoughts you've had for many, many years. But after only four months or so, you'll notice an upward shift in your self-esteem. You'll also notice a shift in the quality of your wins. They will become easier to recognize and write about, and they will seem more significant and satisfying.

The reason this exercise is so powerful is that the subconscious can be programmed any way you choose. It will always agree with and believe whatever you tell it. During sleep, when your conscious mind is asleep, your subconscious mind is alert.

Most of us go to sleep thinking about the battles we fought that day or the troubles we encountered. We recall the rejections and the slights we suffered, maybe feeling sorry for ourselves. Then we think about how early we have to get up, and rehearse the battles we have to fight the next day. Our subconscious minds process this material all night long.

If you *change the thoughts* you put into your subconscious mind, however, you can reprogram your subconscious. By counting and recording your wins, you let your subconscious help turn you into a winner while you sleep. When this is done over an extended period of time, say a year, you can gain control over your own motivation.

Gary was a real estate agent who was suffering from a market slump, just as most of the agents in his city were. Then he began to celebrate his wins. At first it wasn't easy. Some days, in order to come up with ten wins, he even had to write down: "Got out of bed this morning!" as a win. But gradually things began to improve, and he ended up having the best sales year he ever had—and in a down market.

Joy was a human "hideout." She was the sort of person whose entire appearance communicated one thing: "Don't look at me!" Her clothes were baggy, well-worn, and nondescript. Her hair was cut in such a way that it covered most of her face. She wore no makeup.

She was thinking of starting a video production firm, though she hadn't really done anything about it, when she began recording her wins.

Within six months, Joy had undergone a metamorphosis. She looked terrific. She had trimmed down, she wore great clothes and makeup and nail polish. Even her posture was different. She no longer slouched. Her production company was blossoming, and she had begun another business as a beauty consultant.

These dramatic changes in Joy were the results of celebrating wins every day. Sometimes, however, the results of celebrating wins can be more subtle, as in the case of a manager who phoned to say that she couldn't see any real results from doing this exercise. She said she had celebrated her wins faithfully for four months. And she felt she had had no results.

When asked how her life was going, she began to communicate wonderful things. She said that she had been promoted at work into a new department doing exactly what she loved to do. Her boyfriend of many years was going to marry her. And so on.

When asked if she didn't think that celebrating wins had worked after all, she had to laugh at herself. Things had been getting better in such a gradual and subtle way that she hadn't even noticed it until it was pointed out to her.

During the first year of celebrating wins you will discover what winning is for you. No one will see your list except you; you can be truly honest with yourself. Notice if your wins concern your work or your personal life. Perhaps you win more often in your work life, or perhaps you win more in your personal life. If so you might want to pay closer attention to the side of your life that seems neglected.

Up and Down

The day-to-day flow of life is something like a roller coaster. Sometimes you're at the top of the ride. You feel as if you could sell anybody anything. These are the days when everything goes well, days in which you win without even thinking about it. You're at your peak, the top of the roller coaster, the top of your form.

Then there are the days when your self-esteem is at its lowest. These are the days when you want only to go back to bed and put your head under the pillow. The very idea of work is unappealing. You find yourself being defensive, drawing arguments and unpleasant situations your way. You accuse everyone *else* of being on the defensive. You feel like a victim, and you act that way.

When you celebrate wins, the roller coaster becomes gentler. You'll still have ups and downs, but the *scale* will change. After you faithfully celebrate wins for about four months, your self-esteem will swing between a scale of say, a ten and a three—ten being the high point and three being the low point of your ride.

Eventually, the low days will not be as low. After you celebrate wins for about a year, your self-esteem will swing between a ten and a seven. Your low days will never be as low as they once were. In fact, your low days a year from now will be what you would consider a *good* day today.

As you observe the areas in which you win most often, you will find clues to what your real passion is. You'll also become sensitive to when you're living your passion and when you aren't.

The shift to total self-motivation may take several years.

During this time continue to record your wins. You'll find yourself becoming more powerful, more effective, and more in charge of your life. You'll find that the more wins you can celebrate, the more people who also win will be drawn to you. Celebrating wins is the simplest and most effective way to create a win/win life.

Passion Makes the Difference

People who live their passion are people who make a real contribution to the world. It is difficult, if not impossible, to contribute anything of value to others if you do not give to yourself as well.

People who work their passion are not stuck in limitations, whether self-imposed or imposed by society. In fact, people who work their passion are often considered *outrageous*. Because they have a good time. They love themselves. They live in another dimension, so to speak—beyond the norm, beyond the status quo.

Passion doesn't mean being unreasonable or wild. It means possessing strength and power. It means transcending fear and hostility. Passion means winning just by *doing what you do*. And by being who you are.

7

Time

TIME IS ONE of those concepts we use all the time—no pun intended!—without really knowing what it means.

Consider how many ways we use the word:

"Time is on my side."

"I'm out of time."

"Time's a-wasting."

"All in good time."

"I never have enough time."

"Be on time."

And finally, the question we ask ourselves or others time and time again: "What time is it?"

The fact is, nobody knows what time *really* is—not the people who are always saving it or running out of it, or the scientists and philosophers who think in terms of abstruse concepts such as infinity and the space/time continuum. Time is all around us, but it remains a mystery.

There is, however, one definite thing we do know about time. We can always come up with an answer to the question, "What time is it?" And we can always answer it in the same way.

No matter who or what or where we are, the answer is always the same. It is always "Now."

The Only Time There Is

Now is the only time we have. This very moment is the only moment we live in. No one has ever lived two moments at once. Now you're living this moment, and now you're living this next moment. The moment you're living is always new because it's always changing. And everyone always has the same amount of time—which is *now*.

There's a cartoon in which Dennis the Menace is watching his father set the grandfather clock in the living room. He asks his father, "Dad, isn't it always now?"

Nadine Stair, an eighty-one-year-old woman, wrote an essay called "If I Had My Life to Live Over." She said, "Oh, I've had my moments, and if I had to do it over again, I'd have more of them. In fact, I'd try to have nothing else. Just moments, one after another, instead of living so many years ahead of each day."

The wonderful thing about the present moment is that it is always changing; you can create each moment anew and live it as you choose. The only thing that gets in the way of our doing that is our habit of living in the past and the future.

The Ghost of Time Past

Our minds are haunted by the past, by memories of things that once happened, which we tend to repeat like an endless tape or broken record. We have all had different experiences, of course, and we all have different pasts, but there are some basic categories—a few particular ghosts—which we can all learn to recognize. And to see through.

The Ghost of This-Is-the-Way-It-Has-Always-Been

In this case, we want the present moment, whatever we are doing now, to conform to expectations based upon how things used to be. But external conditions *now* are always different from what they were in the past.

Knowledge is important and invaluable. "He who cannot remember the past is condemned to repeat it," is how the philosopher George Santayana put it. But to *learn* from the past is one thing; to *live* there is quite another.

The Ghost of Old-Tapes-Never-Lie

We are each a product of our past experiences and environments. These past experiences are recorded in our minds like old tapes, and have in many instances become associated with strong emotions. These "tapes" constitute our conditioning to behave a certain way.

A simple example is this: If you were once bitten by a dog, you may have a tape inside you that tells you *dogs bite.* When you are near a dog today—years or even decades after you were bitten—you might find yourself frightened, even if the dog is a harmless, cute little puppy. But the actual nature of this dog makes no difference to you, because you hear the sound of an old tape—in the present.

A young saleswoman for a major computer firm noticed that occasionally a customer would remind her of her father. She found that when she made sales calls on these customers she would behave as she had as a thirteen-year-old speaking with her father. Naturally, she didn't make a particularly good impression on her would-be customers. Nor did she make many sales.

Becoming aware of the sound of old tapes is a crucial part of learning to live in present time, as is realizing that the old tapes no longer necessarily speak the truth. Just because something was true for you in the past, it does not follow that it is still true for you today.

The Ghost of Emotions Past

From the win/win perspective, the emotions of fear and anger (along with their derivatives—resentment, guilt, and the desire for revenge), when they are inappropriate and unproductive, are powerful barriers to living in the present. Often these emotions aren't based in the present, on what is happening now, but are echoes of past experiences.

Emotions are basically psychic energy. Energy is neutral, neither good nor bad. It just *is*. This is just as true for so-called "negative" emotions as it is for positive emotions.

When we experience negative emotions such as fear and anger, we feel uncomfortable, and we naturally look for ways to discharge or "get rid of" these emotions. One way to do that is to turn the energy of the emotion inward, against ourselves. There are many ways to do this. Some people drink or use drugs in a self-destructive manner; others simply get depressed, or get sick, or become apathetic. Some people might overeat, or punish themselves by *not* eating. In any case, the point is that much self-destructive behavior is the result of anger or fear turned inward.

When people recognize this, they often decide that it is better to "express" their emotions. But still they recognize that it might be harmful to express them to other people. So they take their emotions out on *things* instead. They might take a tennis racket and smash it on the bed, or they might pound their fists on a pillow, or scream and holler in a closed room.

While such strategies for dealing with negative emotions are understandable, they're not conducive to winning—either for oneself or with others. The win/win way of dealing with negative emotions is to recognize, first of all, that emotions are *energy*, and then to recognize that all emotions, like coins, have two sides. The opposite side of the coin of fear is power, for example, and the opposite side of the coin of anger is creativity.

When you live in the past, you're stuck staring at one side of the coin. But when you live in the present moment, you can first of all recognize the pure energy of the negative emotion you're experiencing, and then transform it into its opposite. To transform energy into its most positive form, you must be living in the present. Leave the past and your attachment to the emotion that comes from the past, and move into the present. Then your point of view can be free and unbiased by the past. Only in the present can you freely choose to transform one emotion into another.

The Ghost of Time to Come

Ghosts can haunt the future as well as the past often with similar effects. They both can make you *miss your life*.

When we plan for the future, we tend to live for the future. We live for the day Prince or Princess Charming arrives in a white Porsche, for the day when we get the big promotion, when we "make it," when we get married, when we get divorced, when we have children, when the children are gone, when we win the lottery, when we really get to work, when we take our vacation. We all have our "when" lists, and they're all different. But they all have one thing in common: they tend to be endless.

In Eugene O'Neill's famous play, "The Iceman Cometh," a barroomful of dreamers sit nursing their drinks and waiting for a mysterious man named Hickey to arrive. Each person is certain that when Hickey arrives all of their pipe dreams will become reality. When Hickey finally does arrive, he turns out to be a traveling salesman with a glad hand and a ready smile—and with absolutely no ability to fulfill anybody's dreams. The people waiting in the bar are understandably disillusioned and angry—but they should have known better. Hickey is not to blame.

In the play, Hickey finally did arrive even if he didn't bring anybody's dreams along. His presence did create a kind of meeting-ground for the present and the future, though. In the real world, however, "Hickey"—tomorrow—never comes. As the saying goes, "You never know how things will turn out." This is true for all of us. The future is always unknown. No one has the edge of knowing what will or will not happen.

Rather than living in the future, stay focused on the opportunities and possibilities of every moment. Only then, by living in the *now*, will your win/win future be assured.

The Trouble with Time Management

Time-management courses are valuable for what they can teach us about using time effectively and efficiently through setting priorities in our lives.

Yet most people who have ever taken a time-management course eventually figure out that they still can't really manage time. Even if you have every minute of every day filled with "to do" lists, and you complete every item on your list, you might still find that the day was wasted. How many new opportunities and possibilities did you miss because you were blindly sticking to your list—to your idea of what you *should* be doing? How did you handle all the *unplanned* situations that came up? And finally, how did you benefit from all these lists and plans? Did you take time just to *be*?

Time-management systems work—up to a point. But their limitations are very real. How can you *plan* the most important things in life, things like falling in love, magical moments with your children, hugging babies, listening to a friend? These things happen when they happen, no matter how detailed and "prioritized" your planning is.

Have you ever noticed that you always somehow have enough time for the things you *really* want to do? When you find that you don't have time for something, it's usually because that thing is not important enough. It's lower on your list of priorities than the things that really matter.

Goal-setting is another important technique of time-management. Goal-setting can be valuable because it spurs us to take action. Yet it's doubtful that even half the goals set by businesses or individuals are ever met. Think of all the reams of "annual strategic plans" that sit yellowing and crumbling in the backs of filing cabinets, while the real business is taking place on a moment-to-moment basis— and you will have a good idea of the role that goals actually play in business.

If we look closely at the *reality* of goals we see that there are two very different types of goals.

First there are the goals we set which we absolutely *know* we will meet. These are based upon living and working our passion, and are the natural outcome of our being and our self-expression.

Then there are the goals we set because we think we should. For example, probably the most common goal is to make lots of money. Such a goal is often not attained—the reason being that you didn't *really* want that goal but you thought you should want it. When you set goals according to "should" instead of your real desire or need, the very act of setting a goal can get you off the track of following your real passion. These goals are by their very nature limiting. Think of how much better you might do if you didn't give yourself such self-defeating goals.

Goal-setting is a place to start, not a place to end up. If you find setting goals helpful, as many people do, then by all means set them—until you realize you no longer need them. Then you will be free to live in the present.

Rather than trying to manage their time by constantly consulting "to do" and goal-setting lists, people who live the win/win way ask themselves, "What wants to happen now?" And then they let that happen.

The Flesh and Blood of Present Time

All of us have experienced intense moments of *nowness*—a moment when time seemed to slow down, speed up, or even stop.

Some of us experience this moment of *present* time during athletics, especially during the exhilaration of peak performance, or while skiing, hiking, or wind-surfing. For others it comes during moments of playing with children or with pets. At these times, hours can seem like minutes, or minutes like hours. Sometimes this sense of "this moment is the only moment there is" happens when you fall madly in love, and sometimes it happens while making love.

Such moments of present time are magical. They are also elusive. While we can't "make" such moments happen, we can practice certain exercises that will help us to open up to the present.

The first thing you can do is to simply recall for yourself a time when you had a peak experience or felt yourself living fully in the present. Remember that moment in complete detail. Recall the sound you heard, what you saw, what the weather felt like. Relive the emotions and feelings you had at the time. Remember if there were any special fragrances or if there was a taste you can vividly recall.

Now, answer these questions:

Were you worried or anxious?

Were you afraid?

Did you care what others said or thought?

Did you feel a sense of communion with others (if present)?

Were you defensive or attacking?

Were you emotionally attached to the outcome?

Were you in a state of resistance and struggle and effort?

Did you feel extraordinarily happy?

Did you feel a sense of living in eternity?

Your answers to these questions can give you some sense of what being in present time feels like.

Another exercise to help you live in present time is called "Take Time Out to Take Time In." This "time out" is similar to the "time out" kids or athletes take during games— except that this "time out" is time you take out to spend in personal contemplation and attunement. Paradoxically, when you take this time out you will find that you have even *more* time to get things done in your life—because you will be living the time spent *in* work or other activities more fully. You will be more focused, more alert, more *present*.

There are many ways to take time out. Time-out activities might be meditation or exercise. Hiking, cross-country skiing, sewing, flower arranging, dancing, gardening, knitting, fishing, woodworking, cooking, or yoga can all be used as time out.

All of these activities have certain elements in common. They are quiet. They are solitary, for the most part. Quiet plus solitary means that they are contemplative.

Contemplative activities take place in present time. They are engaged in for their own sake—not to produce or accomplish something else. Contemplative activities, time-outs, are means, not ends. In Zen Buddhism, it is said that such activities are *purposeless*. They have no point other than the process of doing (or not doing!) them. If you sew for your own enjoyment, and happen to produce beautiful clothing, then you could say this was a contemplative time-out activity. But not if you're sewing to make a living or rushing to complete a dress for an upcoming party.

If you exercise or "work out" as a way to "sweat out the demons" and relax, that qualifies as a true time out—but not if you work out to compete and win, or to lose weight. Losing weight is usually a highly emotionally-charged issue, and your participation in exercise for this purpose would probably involve a fair amount of stress. Present-time activities work best when they do not include emotionally-charged issues or goals.

Present-time activities are not mere diversions. A diversion is fun, but it doesn't have that solitary, contemplative quality. Playing cards, going shopping, going to a party, or watching TV or movies are all diversions. They are fun, but they are not true time-out or present-time activities.

How much time-out time should you take? Basically, you

start with whatever feels comfortable for you. It could be as little as five minutes a day. (You don't want this to become another "should" in your life, after all.) But it's suggested that you eventually get to the point where you can allow yourself to "goof off" with quality activities for one and a half hours each day. This may sound like much too much. But many people find that the more time they take off, the more time they have.

One well-known Hollywood actor chants for an hour and a half twice a day. That makes three hours a day! But he insists that he now has much more time than he had before. Many others who have entered into the ritual of present-time activities have had the same experience. Want more time? Take time out to take time in.

This suggestion can be frightening for people who have never taken quiet time for themselves. A manager of a ski store, for example, objected that he had never done anything like this before. He asked if talking to friends on the telephone qualified—which, of course, it doesn't. (Not solitary, not quiet, to begin with.) He then thought about getting in his car, and just driving around, because he loved to drive. That might qualify, although it's probably not an activity that he would do on a daily basis.

As you get into the habit of taking some time out every day, you will begin to notice a difference in the quality of your work and happiness. You will get more done with more energy. You will find that you are automatically transforming your energy into its highest form.

The results will be subtle—just as the results of celebrating wins, which we introduced earlier, are subtle. It may take a month before you notice any difference, and it may take as long as a year before the results are obvious. But remember, *you are worth it.* The win/win way does not really require work. It requires devotion—to yourself and to others. Taking time out is a very loving thing to do for yourself.

Don't Get Stuck

Taking time out will help you develop two special qualities that are very important for success on the win/win way. These qualities are *detachment* and *non-resistance*.

Detachment means that you are not emotionally attached to the outcome of encounters. Another way of saying it is that you can approach life with calm and grace. Detachment doesn't mean that you are cold-blooded or lacking in compassion. It means that the quality of your self-esteem and self-caring is high enough that you know you will be all right regardless of the outcome of any situation.

Non-resistance grows out of an attitude of detachment, and is *the* most powerful form of interaction. Non-resistance means that you let your life unfold, you "go with the flow." We can learn much about how non-resistance works by looking at water. Water always conforms to its surroundings; it is equally at home in a cup or a lake. Water doesn't resist being water, and as the saying goes, it always seeks its own level.

But that doesn't mean that water is somehow weak or ineffectual. In fact, water is probably the most powerful element there is. Water carves rock and cuts deep gorges and canyons. Water literally moves mountains. Non-resisting water carved the Grand Canyon, and non-resisting water carries a half-million tons of silt out of the Grand Canyon each day. Gentle water teaches us the awesome power of non-resistance.

The present moment has the same sort of power. It is the present moment, drop by drop, that cuts the canyons of the past and carves out the mountains and rivers of our future. The present moment is always quiet and still, if we can be quiet and still enough to know it, but that same quietness and stillness contains nothing less than the awesome power of our life.

Present-time Rewards

Let's take a look at the benefits of living fully in the present.

1. First, the present time is its own reward. *To be where you are when you are there* is the only way to be happy.

The present time is a time of self-actualization. Alvin Jones, a psychologist at Cumberland Mental Health Center in North Carolina, and Rick Crandall, editor of the *Journal of Social Behavior and Personality*, who have developed a new index of self-actualization, find that people who are truly self-actualizing are what they call "time competent." They live in the present, rather than in the past with guilts and regrets, or in the future with over-idealized goals or fear.

2. The present time is *a time of no stress*. Living in the present is the perfect stress-reduction tool. Stress comes from living in the future and from living in the past, from feeling that you have too much to do and not enough time in which to do it. By living in the present time, you will have more time to do what you want to do.

3. The present moment is *a time of high intuition*. Intuition is available to everyone by tuning into every moment—by noticing what you are sensing, and what signals your body, heart, and mind are sending you. Intuition— the proverbial sixth sense—is masked when you do not live in the present moment.

4. It is only in the present moment that we can *find the win/win alternative*, that we can choose win/win over win/lose. It is difficult, if not impossible, to find the win/win alternative when you're functioning in the past or in the future.

5. *Concentration* is a function of present time. Kurt Vonnegut, Jr. says that the single most important factor in being successful is the ability to concentrate. Focus is essential. Focus and concentration are present time activities.

6. *Knowing how to listen* is also an important part of any win/win relationship, either business or personal. Genuine

listening can take place only in present time. To truly listen to someone—to hear what they are saying as opposed to what you *think* they are saying or what you *want* them to be saying—it is necessary to put aside all your judgments and preconceptions, and to simply focus on the other person.

7. Present time is the *place of presence*—of being present. The most valuable gift you can give someone is your presence. Material gifts are valuable too, but if we never give our full focus and presence to another person, the gift becomes meaningless.

8. *Connection to others* takes place in present time. The ability to relate to others, and to give of ourselves, is a present-time activity. Connection to others comes about when you are able to focus on others in a present-time way.

9. *Disputes are resolved* in the present time. Most arguments result from being stuck in either the past or future. Disputes are usually disagreements about what did or did not happen in the past. Or about expectations of the future. Phrases like "You said . . ." or "You always . . ." or "I don't believe you'll do . . ." are clues that the dispute is taking place in another time. If you can focus on the present you can often break an impasse.

10. *Personal power* is a function of living in the present moment. If you want to be powerful, you must be powerful in the present. The present moment is your point of power. It is the moment you can make a choice in favor of a win/win solution. *Now* is the moment of choice.

Don't Forget

There is only the present. The past is a present moment that has gone and is remembered. The future is a present moment that has not yet arrived and is imagined. The *now* is available to everyone. Always.

8

Team

THE FIRST TWO win/win keys of passion and time directly relate to the first half of the win/win equation—to *your* winning.

The third and final win/win key is *team*. Team-thinking brings the other side of the win/win equation into play. Team-thinking is what makes it possible for the other person to win along with you. Your winning will thus include others, will include more than yourself, so that when you win you will win in a bigger way. *Team* means that your winning will multiply and increase exponentially. Team-thinking is the natural result of living passion in your work and living in the present time. It is the *dynamic* aspect of the win/win way.

Whose Team Are You On?

Remember when you were a kid, and it came time to choose a team for baseball, Cowboys and Indians, Capture the Flag, or whatever? Usually the more skillful or aggressive or popular players were chosen first—and naturally everybody wanted to be on the "best" team, the winning team. Being the last one picked to play was a painful experience for many kids, and not being picked to play at all—not being "on the team"—could be a crushing experience.

From the conventional point of view, the one most of us have grown up with, team means exclusivity. First of all, a team by standard definition excludes those people who are not on the team, the ones who weren't "good enough" and couldn't "make the team." Often this sort of exclusivity exists even within the team. Some players are better than others, we think, and so we see some parts of a team as better than other parts. This process soon creates divisiveness within a team—the very opposite of the reason the team was formed in the first place.

Second, the conventional notion of a team is that you exclude the other team or teams. The other team, by definition, is the opponent. Your team excludes other teams by beating them.

The win/win notion of team is very different. From the win/win point of view, team is defined as inclusive rather than exclusive, as you-and-me rather than as you-or-me. Win/win teams include *everybody*.

What this means is that, from the win/win point of view, we recognize that we are not just members of one team which opposes other teams. We are—potentially—members of *everybody's* team.

The secret of creating a win/win team is that you can do it all by yourself. You don't need other people to agree with you, or even to consciously join with you. You simply align yourself with them in supporting their highest good, and in the expression of that good. This is your choice.

In other words, you can always make the first move in the win/win game a move of cooperation by supporting others and by aligning yourself with them. You can join anybody's team simply by doing it. The other person doesn't even need to know or agree that you are on his team. The first move is always up to you, and it should always be a move of cooperation. This is an important principle of win/win strategy.

In this way you can enroll yourself on absolutely everybody's team—on your manager's team, on your employee's team, on your co-worker's team, on your husband's team or your wife's team or your children's team or your partner's team. The possibilities are endless, and could, some day, grow to include everyone in the entire world.

But there is no need to wait for that. You can begin in the smallest way, with the person next to you. You can create a you-and-me team with the people standing next to you at the elevator by something as seemingly inconsequential as holding the door open for them, or by asking them which floor they want when you press the button. You can create a team with those drivers who want your spot on the highway by allowing them to pass. If you are standing in the express line at the check-out counter in the supermarket, and the person in front of you has twenty items, you can join that person's team by not getting angry or upset.

After all, if you are *determined* to be on other people's team, and if you are *determined* to make them successful, how can they stop you? Even if they find a way to prevent you from doing anything with them on the concrete level, you can still sincerely wish them well.

It may seem impractical or outrageously idealistic or even bizarre to enroll on teams with all those around you, including people you don't even like. But the point to remember is that we've all found ourselves in rough situations with "sharks" and other win/lose characters. And most of us, at one time or another, have been the shark—and we now realize that sharks sometimes have serious problems relating with others. Yet extraordinary things can happen when people have the courage and daring to create win/win teams by themselves. You-and-me team thinking does work, and work very well. Which is what makes it worth doing.

Teams That Work

In 1981, the Ford Motor Company's plant in Sharonville, Ohio, was producing the worst truck transmissions in the entire country. At any point in time they had five hundred labor grievances pending against them. Employee attitude toward management could best be summed up by this quote: "Anyone who wore a tie we did not trust." The company, not surprisingly, was seriously contemplating closing the plant.

At that time, the company implemented a program called "Employee Involvement." Its purpose was to solve quality-control problems. Every week, management and blue-collar workers met in teams to discuss possible solutions to the plant's problems. This was in itself a big step since it forced workers and management to *talk* with each other.

Interestingly enough, it was more difficult for the executives and managers to sit down and talk with union workers than it was for the workers to talk in groups with management. In any case, much re-education was necessary on both sides. At first, "re-education" meant getting rid of assumptions that had built up over the years. But it also meant that both sides had to change their personal definitions of what "team" meant. Both sides had to recognize that rather than being members of opposing teams, they were in fact members of the same team. They were all in it together: if plant quality and production did not improve, the plant would be closed.

Within four years, quality was up sixty percent, and the number of labor grievances at any point in time was reduced to fifty—which meant, among other things, that management was spending far less time and paperwork on labor problems. One result of the new spirit of teamwork and cooperation was that the executive cafeteria was transformed into a exercise area for the use of all the employees—and the executives now took their meals in the employee cafeteria along with everyone else.

Ten years ago a group of women called the Women Business Owners Association went to Washington to lobby for more small-business loans for women, and for increased recognition of their plight. They adopted a militaristic, confrontational, aggressive approach. And they went home empty-handed. When they regrouped to consider their next step, they decided that they hadn't treated the politicians and bureaucrats as part of the same team they—the women business-owners—were on. They adopted a new strategy, which they called "the velvet, silk, and pearls confrontational guerilla tactics," and returned to Washington, where this time they were much more successful. They convinced the government that the small-business loans they wanted would benefit the national economy as a whole and not "just women." Today, incidentally, women own and operate one out of every four small businesses.

Agreement

There are several levels of team and teamwork. The first is the level of *agreement*, where all members of the team have come to agreement about their common purpose. For many people, this is the sole criterion for a team. If team members cease to agree, then the team no longer exists.

It's important to be clear about the first level of agreement. Most people feel that they have to be in agreement with their boss or manager or the people who work with them, in order to make a situation work—but at the same time few of us ever stop to think about which *specific* areas there should be agreement in. You may decide, for example, that you can agree on the basic purpose of a business, but that you will not work for a company that asks you to lie, steal, or cheat. In other words, you may decide that you will only work with people who agree with you about basic ethics. Many misunderstandings and difficulties could have been avoided if people had been clear about the im-

portant areas of agreement *before* they began working together.

On the other hand, it is inevitable that people who work
or live together will have disagreements. It is highly unlikely—or even desirable—that people will agree about
everything. Each of us is unique. Each of us has our own
personal values and beliefs. Because we all think differently it's natural for disagreement to arise. If we all wel-
comed and honored our uniqueness, we would also be able
to welcome our disagreements. But this is not the case.
People tend to think that everyone should think the way
they do.

Agreements are necessary for a team to work, but it's
important to recognize that first-level agreements are made
at a very basic and limited level. The agreement between
the members of a baseball team, for example, is a simple
agreement that all the players are playing to win baseball
games. But the players may not agree at all, for example,
on the *strategy* for winning particular games. Agreement,
therefore, is not necessarily a basis for lasting harmony
within a team.

Alignment

The second level of team is called *alignment*. At this level it
is possible that you could disagree with someone and still
be on his team. Alignment around a common goal allows
for agreement and disagreement to co-exist. The basic criterion for alignment isn't that all members must agree, but
that all members align themselves around a common vision. In other words, they all want the same "superordi-
nate" results—the highest results they're all aiming for. For
example, members of a team might be aligned around a
vision of a company's success, or raising a family, or hon-
oring a particular spiritual discipline.

In order to attain alignment, then, team members must

have a common goal or vision—which can only be achieved by the collective efforts of aligned individuals. This common purpose allows for the existence of disagreement. The team members don't have to all agree on process and procedures because they have a higher, overriding goal.

This goal is never money. It usually has to do with serving others, with making a difference in the world. Though this goal reaches beyond individual gain, it also *includes* individual gain. If individual gain is not included, then alignment cannot take place—which is why finding and working your passion is such an essential first step.

The Power of Disagreement

At the alignment level, disagreement can work as a very powerful tool. When people always agree, or agree too easily, things can become wrongly "smoothed over." Disagreement and conflict can create new insights and combinations of ideas. Disagreement within an aligned team can actually accelerate the solution-making process.

At the first level of agreement, there is often a bias toward superficial concordance, since agreement is all that is holding the team together. Many first-level agreements are thus compromises or false agreements, which will later erupt and sabotage the team.

In alignment, however, all members have the freedom to be who they really are, to express their true thoughts, to voice their opinions. Alignment makes it possible for members of a team to be free to disagree without worrying that they're destroying the team. This freedom to disagree, to express conflict, is healthy and essential to creating win/win teams. Disagreement in this sense does *not* result in endless conflict. Disagreement in a relationship does not mean "breaking up," or fighting, nor does it result in a standoff. Where there is alignment to a higher goal, disagreement can ultimately result in resolution and harmony at a higher level.

Alignment requires that people respect each other. They do not need to like each other, but mutual respect is necessary. This mutual respect is based upon a recognition that attainment of the common goal or purpose is the reason people are working together.

Working on a team at the level of alignment is rewarding, exciting, and enjoyable. It puts things in perspective. When you work this way, with a larger purpose in mind, you are free to "not sweat the small stuff."

When you move to the level of alignment in your personal and professional relationships you begin to develop a new set of skills and attitudes. The basic point is to change personal *positions* into personal *preferences*. A position is a "hard and fast" line, while a preference is much more flexible. "Taking a position" is much more limiting than "having a preference." When you take a position, you are saying that there is only one possible solution, which is your way. When things can only be your way, you automatically create opposition. Taking a position creates polarities; it creates a battlefield mentality and a battlefield world. Both sides dig in and put up defenses. There is no neutral ground, no free play. Everyone is forced to take *one* position—either for or against.

Having a preference, on the other hand, means that you have the freedom to entertain many opinions, and therefore many solutions. At the same time, because preferences are more flexible than positions, everyone feels that they have the freedom to express their true thoughts and feelings. Positions tend to jeopardize negotiations. Positions must be held; preferences can be changed or modified with little loss of face. Preferences are much more forgiving. Though it might not seem so at first glance, *preferences* are actually more powerful than *positions*, and provide the greatest opportunity for finding the win/win way.

Synergy

The third level of team is called *synergy*. Synergy grows naturally out of alignment. At the synergy level, the whole (once again) is far greater than the sum of individual efforts. At the level of synergy, the effects of individual efforts are multiplied, and the rules of logic no longer necessarily apply. At the level of synergy, magical things happen every day. Synergy can create results that may be ten or a hundred or fifteen thousand times the expected output.

Synergy is not programmable. There are no "ten easy steps" to the level of synergy. Synergy is a way of being, a form of energy; it is the attunement to a high order of harmony within the whole—in this case, within the whole team.

Businesses that can function at the level of synergy can confound all expectations. One example is the Group, a real estate company in Fort Collins, Colorado. The Group is one of the most successful real estate companies in the country, despite its somewhat unlikely location.

The Group, as its name implies, is based upon *team* and *synergy* at a very high level. Everybody who works at the Group, from the janitor and the receptionist to the top-selling salesperson, is a part owner of the Group. Thus everybody has a share—and a stake—in everybody else's success. "Because of the ownership structure, we have internal cooperation," notes salesman Don Svitak. "There's not the competition among salespeople which seems to be the standard in the industry. By becoming partners, we're willing to share. We have no 'salesman of the month,' no plaques, no awards that distinguish one salesman from the rest. We don't believe that is the way to motivate salespeople; we motivate them by their sense of purpose."

In many sales-oriented businesses, people hoard leads and clients. In effect, they hoard information. But when people work at the level of synergy, as they do in the Group, they realize that sharing information adds up to increased results for everyone. At the level of synergy, adding your information to everyone else's information creates a *higher* level of information—from which everyone can profit.

"The key is having a large in-house inventory of listings, combined with an environment of alignment and communication among our partners so that they're talking to one another," explains Group founder and president Larry Kendall. What this means is that buyer and seller are frequently both represented by a member of the Group. Fully seventy percent of the Group's transactions take place completely within the Group.

Synergy, as we have said, cannot be programmed. It is the result of an inner attitude, a win/win attitude. Unless it comes from within, from truly wanting others to win, it won't work. Synergy exists at the Group because the Group members consciously develop and maintain a win/win attitude. They pay attention to their own well-being, to begin with, by spending time at least once a week on self-improvement, such as participating in "human potential" training programs. They make their own development and growth part of their business. In terms of the win/win way, they make sure that all members of the Group are discovering and developing their passion.

"There are a lot of reasons to be here besides the fact that you do more business being with the top firm," says Kendall. "People who work here are working in a learning, growing environment. Why would anyone want to go to work anywhere where they couldn't learn something? I see a lot of real estate people making career decisions based on the commission split, without really asking themselves, 'What about my personal growth and development, and what am I really going to learn there?' They also fail to consider what that company has to offer the customer— what can that company offer the customer that's unique and different?"

"One of the reasons that anybody comes to the Group is Larry," says salesperson Bobbie Cook. "He's always working on the edge. He's brilliant at going to seminars and coming back and giving us the flavor of it in thirty minutes. You can call it skimming, but we really benefit from it. I won't miss a sales meeting if I'm in town because they're so good."

At sales meetings, humanistic disciplines such as neuro-linguistic programming are used to demonstrate the company motto which is "NO LIMITS." Firewalking and karate board-breaking with bare hands have also been used. "We've had eighty-five-pound women who can break a board with their bare hands and two-hundred-pound men who can't," says Kendall. "During this training process people do four guided visualizations. In one of them they communicate with their subconscious and get it totally aligned. There are really two people inside of us—one says, 'I know I can do this,' and another says, 'Oh no you can't; I bet you can't. What would happen if you get hurt?' It's that little voice that keeps a lot of people from achieving their potential. So this training is not about breaking wood; the wood-breaking is a metaphor for internal alignment, getting focused and seeing that you can do something that, an hour before, seemed impossible."

This is probably the reason that no company has succeeded in duplicating the Group's success, even though a number of companies have tried to adopt the Group's philosophy and operating principles. "The concept is very intriguing to real estate people," says Larry Kendall. "They come here and they want to learn the concept in an hour over lunch. And then they run out and self-destruct. The mechanical structure is there to support a belief system and an environment that is closely nurtured by the management and the board of directors. You've got to have that piece too; you can't just have the structure. People start using the clout of their ownership to promote their own personal goals, to the detriment of the other people or the corporation. Ultimately it will be worse for those people than working in an oppressive, autocratic type of company."

In fact, Larry Kendall gives many talks in which he freely discloses what others would ordinarily consider proprietary information. He explains very specifically how to do what the Group has done. But the secret of the Group's success is not to be found in blindly following the Group's operating principles. It depends upon each person, each team member, walking on the win/win path—and then joining with others to develop the synergy that makes the Group work.

Indeed, the Group is very careful to accept only those who are aligned with the Group's purpose. "When we interview somebody, we look for alignment and passion. We look to see if they're aligned with our values, our goals, our culture, our belief system, and the way we do business. We look for someone who can add value to us while we add value to them."

Kendall cites a real estate agent who wanted to work for the Group. He had made $200,000 the year before. "You'd normally kill to have a $200,000 producer," says Kendall. "But the way he did it was to trade some condos in Vail for an oil well in Oklahoma, and he was selling a farm in Nebraska. He could have come to work with us and he would have done real well. But there wouldn't have been any synergy created because we wouldn't have been in the same niche, aligned, doing the same things."

Synergy can disintegrate rapidly when team members don't stay focused on their mission and work at levels *beyond* agreement. Often such synergy naturally dissolves when the purpose has been completed. It can also happen when your passion leads you into a new situation.

A good example of how synergy can disintegrate is the famous split of the partners who originally developed the Apple computer. Stephen Jobs and Steve Wozniak worked together synergistically to create the Apple computer and then to form the company that successfully produced and marketed it. When the project was completed, with extraordinary success, the energy level dropped from synergy to alignment and then to agreement. Finally, Wozniak left the company to pursue new research ideas while Jobs stayed on to finalize the Apple computer.

Some of us might see this as a failure of synergy. But from another point of view the break was perfect. Each partner had fulfilled his passion. It was simply time for the next challenge, for the next opportunity. The end of synergy was the natural by-product of the work they had accomplished.

Teams, like everything else in this world, are not intended to last forever. In fact, the natural flow of a person's self-expression through his passion often precludes everlasting synergy in the same team. It is not unusual for people to join together in synergy to produce something wonderful, and then dissolve the working team.

Synergy requires the members of a team to be individuals who are free to express their passion. Synergy cannot exist when individual members of a team dislike either their work or themselves. It is thus in the best interests of inspired managers and executives to hire people who like themselves and can work their passion.

Embrace Your Tiger

It's easy enough to create a team with people we like and admire, or with whom we share common interests, but what do you do when you find yourself on a team with somebody you don't get along with at all?

We all have somebody who might be termed "the One." The One is the person who'd make your life perfect—if only he'd go away. The One is the one person whose team you absolutely don't want to be on, the one person you don't support and will not support, the one person who's the most difficult for you, the one person who's preventing you from being happy. This is the person who gets in your way, the person you resent, the person you can't stand to be with—let alone be on his team.

Everyone has the One. And everyone wishes they didn't. But if everyone has the One, perhaps, just perhaps, the One is a necessary part of our lives. Perhaps the One is a gift.

The One may be your spouse or your child or your parent. The One may be your boss or your employee or a politician or a leader of a foreign government. The One is the person you want to change, and the person who seems to stand in the way of your getting what you want.

The One is actually your "tiger"—your personal challenge. You cannot change the tiger. You can only change yourself. People change when they *choose* to change, not when you try to convince them to change. They change when they can no longer stand the pain or when they *have* to change in order to get what they want in their life.

Just as you can't change your tiger, you can't run away from your tiger. If you run away from a tiger, the tiger will chase you, overtake you, and devour you. Running away from the tiger can never work. It is never a solution to interpersonal conflict.

For Brent, the tiger was always his boss. Brent was forty-three years old and had been employed in a number of high-level jobs, always for four or five years at a time. He had served in city and county governments, and had been president of several companies.

Brent was, by all appearances, a very successful man. There was only one problem. He left each position after four or five years. When asked what the common ingredient was in all of his departures, he replied, "It's those bosses. They always end up being blankety-blank people. It gets to the point where I can no longer tolerate working for them, so I quit. Occasionally they fire me first."

Then he was asked, "Was there an even more common element than the bosses?"

Brent couldn't think of one. He was convinced that his bosses were the problem. If only he hadn't had those bosses, the jobs would have been perfect.

There *was,* however, an even more common element. That element was Brent. *He* was always there. He always took *him* with him. That's why every time Brent left a job, the tiger found him again. The tiger may have had a different face, and lived in a different city, but the tiger was the same tiger as before.

Of course, if you fall down in front of a tiger and give up or surrender, the tiger will be very happy to eat you. When you *face* your tiger, you cannot become the tiger's victim; you cannot let yourself be eaten alive. In short, you cannot set yourself up to win if you are running away from your tiger, or if you are surrendering to him.

There is another way, an alternative way, to deal with the tiger. The alternative way is to *embrace* the tiger. When you can do that, you can truly win.

By embracing your tiger, you are accepting your tiger, enjoying your tiger, appreciating your tiger.

Whatever we perceive about another person is always a reflection of ourselves. It is impossible to see a flaw in anyone unless it somehow exists in us. Whenever we judge another person, either in a positive or negative fashion, we are only speaking about ourselves. When we look at another person, we are seeing ourselves reflected in that face. *The tiger in your life is always your mirror.*

This concept may be troublesome—perhaps even infuriating for you. You may not want to even think about it, let alone talk about it with anyone. Because if you accept it as true it means that all those people you dislike so much have something in common with you. It means you are projecting all of the things you do not like about yourself onto them. The children's saying, "It takes one to know one," becomes the bald truth. Your tiger is also *you.* The good news is that when you master your difficulties with your tiger, you also master yourself.

The opposite is also true, by the way. What you like and admire in other people is also a part of you. When you see beauty in another, the beauty you see is a reflection of your own.

These reflections—and our reactions to them—give us the opportunity for personal growth and mastery. Which is one reason other people are so important. They are the yardstick of our mastery over ourselves.

When you're able to create teams with all other people— those you dislike as well as those you like—it means that you have embraced your tiger. You have embraced all parts and aspects of yourself. True harmony—true team—is then possible. You can then feel gratitude toward and deep appreciation for your tiger. And appreciation and resentment cannot exist simultaneously.

At this level of living and understanding, everything we see around us reflects the level of our own mastery. Every problem becomes a gift. You come to view every person and every tiger with open arms, so that they can be embraced and thus mastered.

At the level of mastery, no problem or tiger is left unembraced. Tigers are your gifts. They are your perfect teachers—and your perfect teammates as well.

Two Stories

Sheila was a customer-service representative for a major computer company. She had the worst customers in the entire department. On any good day, Sheila could always find something to be down about. She was so unhappy— and so disliked—that no one wanted to sit next to her at company meetings.

Sheila was suffering from a malaise that's very common in today's world. She didn't know why she was here or what she was doing; she had no purpose or meaning in life. In short, she was afflicted with a condition we might call "spiritual deprivation."

One day Sheila touched bottom. She realized that she was in great pain, and that she couldn't live that way any longer. She decided to do something about it. Sheila's first step was to understand that her tiger was *Sheila*. She didn't like herself, and she certainly didn't love herself. So she started making changes.

Now, Sheila didn't adopt a positive attitude; she didn't look in the mirror in the morning and see an unfriendly face and then correct it by putting on a smile. First, she had to do some hard work. She had to look deep within herself. She had to take a long piercing look at herself. And she had to do it from a place of non-resistance. If she resisted knowing the truth about herself, she wouldn't have been able to change anything at all. She had to be honest with herself about how she behaved and interacted with others. She had to look at herself objectively, even if she didn't like what she saw. This was the hardest part of her "recovery."

After this period of intense "soul searching," Sheila had to make the decision to care about herself—to begin with. She had to decide to see her own beauty, and she had to let the rest of the world see her beauty.

Sheila began by expressing her new outlook in a very simple way. She began signing her letters "Positive regards." Even on days when everything went "wrong"— on bad days—she managed to find something to be grateful for. She found her purpose, and she came alive.

Within a year, her fellow workers at sales meetings were saving a place for her and bringing her coffee. Her customers became the best customers in the department.

Sheila insists that her *customers* changed. But it was really Sheila who changed her customers by embracing her tiger. People treat us the way we treat ourselves. As Sheila became caring and gentle to herself, as she allowed herself to see who she really was, others responded "in kind."

Sheila's willingness to embrace her tiger resulted in a true win/win situation. The corporation she worked for won, her co-workers won, and her customers won. And, of course, Sheila also won. Even people who knew nothing of what had happened or had no direct connection to Sheila won. Sheila's winning spread like the proverbial ripples on a pond.

Nancy was a schoolteacher in Boulder. As a member of a five-person teaching team for learning-disabled children, she specialized in teaching reading.

Nancy loved teaching, but she was flunking school! On Friday, the principal called Nancy into his office and told her that she would be fired within a week if things did not change. The parents had complained that their children were not learning to read, and they said that the parent/teacher conferences with Nancy were worthless. Of the four other teachers on her team, three wouldn't even speak to Nancy. Everyone was losing—the children, the parents, the team, the teachers, the principal, and Nancy.

Nancy went to her counselor—worried, upset, and in shock. She was completely out of present time. The counselor asked her several questions.

"Is teaching your passion?" Nancy's answer was "Yes, definitely."

"How is this perfect mess your perfect opportunity?" the counselor asked.

Nancy was unable to reply. She didn't see that this "perfect mess" was her chance to create perfection, her chance to clean out old belief systems, old attitudes, old assumptions. It was her chance to rid herself of negativity. So to begin, they made a list of ten things Nancy could gain by working *with* her distressing situation.

"Now," the counselor suggested, "list ten ways that your principal is your perfect teacher."

This time Nancy was able to reply—loud and clear. She told the counselor she was crazy.

Nancy couldn't see that her principal was her tiger. Our tigers are our perfect teachers. It's solely up to us whether we perceive our tigers as enemies or teachers.

The counselor suggested that Nancy begin by finding ways she could benefit through her relationship with her principal. As she worked on her list, Nancy was also able to come up with ways in which she could be grateful for him. And as she finally completed her list, she found herself appreciating him—much to her amazement. And appreciation is one of the first important steps to healing a relationship.

"Now," the counselor said, "list ten ways that the team teachers are your perfect teachers."

When they finally completed the two-hour session, Nancy had transformed a formidable mass of anger and hostility into gratitude and appreciation. She was ready to learn from her perfect teachers. She had been uncomfortable and in pain for much of this process, but that was necessary for her to become aware of her opportunities and to take advantage of them.

Nancy went back to school on Monday. She was not fired. In fact, within two weeks, the principal congratulated her on great parent/teacher conferences. She had won over two of the team teachers, although one still refused to speak to her.

Nancy was able to achieve these impressive results by embracing her tiger. When she shifted her attitude toward others, *she* won and *they* won. But the final result was the most impressive. Her teaching became more effective and the children were learning to read.

A Quick Review

The way to create effective win/win teams is to recognize that everyone is your perfect teacher. This often requires a total shift of perception.

We usually believe that we must overcome our enemies. But do we overcome our enemies by destroying them? When we seek to destroy someone, we set in motion an endless cycle of revenge and destruction—which will sooner or later circle back toward us.

But true triumph comes through mastery, not destruction. We master ourselves *and* our enemies when we can see our enemies as our perfect teachers. That is a lasting victory. When we are able to see our enemies as our teachers, we have completely destroyed them—we have destroyed our enemies by turning them into our teachers. What's wonderful is that in this way your former enemy gets to win also. Which is how a win/win team is created.

As Abraham Lincoln once said, *"I destroy my enemy when I make him my friend."*

Part Three
WINNING WITH OTHERS

9

Negotiating the Win/Win Way Together

THE ABILITY TO negotiate is one of the most important tools a person on the win/win way can have. Most of us think of negotiating in terms of business and international diplomacy. But we all negotiate conflicts every day. We negotiate when we pay or put off paying our bills, when we rent an apartment or buy a pair of shoes. We negotiate in our personal and family lives as well—when we decide what movie to go to or when one person cooks dinner in exchange for the other person washing the dishes.

Win/win negotiators don't try to get the best deal for themselves; they try to find an alternative that will be the best deal for all sides.

The authors of the best-selling *Getting to Yes* explain win/win negotiating this way: "If negotiators view themselves as adversaries in a personal face-to-face confrontation, it is difficult to separate their relationship from the substantive problem . . . Each side tends to become defensive and reactive and to ignore the other side's legitimate interests altogether . . . A more effective way for the parties to think of themselves is as partners in a hardheaded side-by-side search for a fair agreement advantageous to each."

And Fred E. Jandt, author of *Win-Win Negotiating*, says, "Win-Win Negotiating—that's my concept for making conflict work in which parties summon all their imaginative skills and resources to provide each other with an array of beliefs that neither would realize were it not for the other."

Conflict Positive and Negative

Conflict is a fact of life—and a fact of business.

Conflict can erupt at any time, even when both parties are doing their best to work things out in a win/win way.

That's the bad news.

The good news is that the bad news is not necessarily bad. Conflict is not always destructive. In fact, as we have seen, conflict can often be a source of growth, added value, and greater success. But in order for that to happen, conflicts must be seen as possibilities for achieving results that will enhance or improve the disputed situation for *both* parties. In short, conflicts can create the ground for win/win solutions—*if* you learn the basics of negotiating in a win/win way.

First of all, we need to make a distinction between competition and conflict. *Competition* is one particular type of conflict. As we have seen, it implies a zero-sum game in which your loss is my gain, or vice versa. It is also the most negative and unproductive kind of conflict. Competitive conflict causes stress, with all the accompanying physical and psychological discomforts. Competitive conflict within an organization or a relationship leads to a waste of time and energy as individuals jockey for "higher" or "more powerful" positions. It can also result in falling productivity—to what Fred E. Jandt calls "diminished across-the-board performance as parties let the conflict sap them of energy, determination, and dedication."

Productive or positive conflict, on the other hand, is not competitive—though it often appears so at first. Nor is it a zero-sum game—though, again, it often appears so at first.

Positive conflict that's not mere competitiveness can sharpen skills, lead to hitherto unthought-of solutions, stimulate creativity, and inspire people to heights of excellence they might never have even attempted. Positive conflict can also be useful in what might seem to be negative ways: for example, it can expose weaknesses in reasoning or products that might otherwise have gone undetected. Finally, positive conflict can help bring about much-needed social changes. The sit-ins that helped bring about desegregation or the nonviolent campaigns of Gandhi are both examples of positive noncompetitive conflict that led to important social change.

How to Negotiate the Win/Win Way

From the win/win point of view, positive conflict is simply a moment of tension between two sides in an ongoing discussion—a discussion which could result in a higher point of satisfaction for both sides.

To begin with, the win/win negotiator views his or her "opponent" with respect. This means that you assume the other side has *its* reasoning—and that this reasoning is at least as convincing to *them* as yours is to you. It doesn't mean, however, that you "trust" the other side automatically, believe everything they say, and give them everything they want. Rather, you respect your "opponent" in somewhat the same way a martial artist respects his opponent. The martial artist wants to have the most interesting and exciting match possible—for both participants—just as you want to emerge from your negotiations with the best mutually satisfying solution.

To do this you have to know your opponent. Or to be more precise, to do this in negotiations, you must discover what your opponent wants. This might seem easy enough, since most negotiations start out with each side telling the other exactly what they want, but in fact there is often a big difference between what people *think* they want and what they *really* want.

This distinction is the basis of win/win negotiating. It is the difference—to cite the terms used by Roger Fisher and William Ury of the Harvard Negotiating Project, authors of *Getting to Yes*—between *interests* and *positions*. A position, in short, is often what people think they want, while an interest is what they really want. Your job as a win/win negotiator is to find out the interest behind your (or your client's) position, and then to find out the real interest behind your opponent's position—whether your opponent is aware of it or not.

The most direct way to do this is to simply ask questions. Ask *why* your opponent wants that particular sum of money (which you probably think is too high) or that particular corner office (which you probably think is too big, and which you want yourself in any case).

Fisher and Ury present the example of two men sitting in a library—one wanting the window closed, the other wanting the window open—to show the importance of *finding the interest behind the position* in successful negotiating.

On the surface, it seems that the two men are locked in a classic win/lose battle. The window can be *either* open or closed. Each of the men holds the position that he wants what the other does not want.

The librarian-negotiator, however, is a win/win sort of librarian, and so asks each of the gentlemen *why* he wants the window open or shut. One man, it turns out, wants the window closed because he objects to the draft. The other man, it turns out, wants the window open for the fresh air.

The interests (no draft for one, fresh air for the other)

have now become separated from the positions (window shut for one, open for the other). The solution? Open a window in an adjoining room—fresh air for one, no draft for the other.

Finding the underlying interest can often unlock seemingly impossible situations. This point is explained in *Win-Win Negotiating* by Fred E. Jandt, a consultant on conflict-management for organizations like the U.S. Department of Labor, and Xerox. He cites an example of a legal secretary asking for a raise which her boss cannot afford. It might seem useless to ask why in this case: obviously, the secretary wanted more money. And so she did—and for obvious reasons. She needed more money to keep up with her rising expenses.

Her *position* was that she wanted a raise. But her *interest* was that she needed more money. And, as she told her boss (because he took the trouble to ask), she liked her job, which included working on law cases that were *pro bono* (for the public good)—which was, by the way, why her boss couldn't afford to give her a raise.

But he could help her obtain her real interest. As it turned out, she was willing to do some part-time work to get the extra money she needed, and her boss suggested that she take on word-processing for lawyers he knew, using the word-processor in the office. And he agreed to give her a raise as soon as he could afford it.

Here's another example, one from the world of international politics: the Israelis and the Egyptians both held non-negotiable positions about the Golan Heights, which Israel had occupied after the Six-Day War. The Egyptians demanded the return of the land, which they considered Egyptian territory. The Israelis refused. Exploring the interests behind the positions, negotiators discovered that the Egyptians were concerned with national sovereignty, while the Israelis were concerned with security. They didn't want Egyptian missiles and guns in range of Israeli settlements.

The answer was to turn the disputed territory into a demilitarized zone which would be under the Egyptian flag.

Positions, as you see, tend to be either/or, win/lose, open-or-shut propositions. Positions tend to be zero-sum sorts of games. Positions are singular: you take a stand on a position, and then you defend it—no matter what.

But interests are a different matter. They are not as "solid" as positions. You might have one position to defend, but you might have many different ways to obtain your interests. And chances are good that you can find new and creative ways to satisfy both your interests and your opponent's interests.

Brainstorming

How can you find ways to satisfy both your interests and the interests of your opponents?

Coming up with what Fisher and Ury call "options for mutual gain" is a part of negotiating that is often overlooked, but is crucial for the win/win negotiator.

"Too many negotiations end up with half an orange for each side, instead of the whole fruit for one and the whole peel for the other," say the Harvard negotiators.

Coming up with options helps both sides see that you're not dealing with a "fixed pie." Therefore it makes sense for you to help the other side see their options—their different interests—as well. This means putting yourself in the other side's place, trying to see what the world, or at least the problem, looks like to them. It means, in short, *looking for ways for them to win.*

Win/lose negotiations do not generate options. They generate either/or choices that tend to narrow rather than widen the possibilities. Breaking this structure is not easy but it can be done. Brainstorming, for example, is a method in which you suspend your "judgment" for the moment and allow your imagination free rein. Make a list of all the possibilities, and don't worry about their appropriateness for the moment. In fact, it's *better* if you allow yourself to be ridiculous or outrageous since that will free your imagination! Allow yourself to write down everything that comes to mind—from "hire a hit man to take care of the problem" to "give them all they want, including an extra thousand." Then, and only then, is it time to go over your list and decide which options are the best for you.

It's also worth considering brainstorming *with* the other side—but doing it in such a way that nobody is bound or constrained by the options that come up during the brainstorming session. Keep the joint brainstorming as informal and playful as possible. Try getting together in a different setting—at a café or over drinks or at a picnic. If you're in an office, try sitting at a round table, or, if there are two of you, try sitting next to each other, side by side, instead of facing each other, like adversaries, across a table.

Once you've uncovered the interests behind the positions, and brainstormed multiple options, you are ready to negotiate in earnest by identifying—and possibly trading off—shared interests.

Fisher and Ury emphasize three points about shared interests: "First, shared interests lie latent in every negotiation . . . Ask yourself: Do we have a shared interest in preserving our relationship? What opportunities lie ahead for cooperation and mutual benefit? What costs would we bear if negotiations broke off? Are there common principles, like a fair price, that we can both respect?

"Second, shared interests are opportunities, not godsends. To be of use, you need to make something out of them. It helps to make a shared interest explicit and to formulate it as a shared goal . . .

"Third, stressing your shared interests can make the negotiation smoother and more amicable. Passengers in a lifeboat afloat in the middle of the ocean with limited rations will subordinate their differences over food in pursuit of their shared interest in getting to shore."

What About the Bad Guys?

What can you do when you find yourself up against some-body who's playing a "hardball" win/lose game, the sort of person who stakes out a position, digs in, and says, "Take it or leave it"? The first thing you can do is spend a few hours with the two books that we have referred to in this chapter: *Getting to Yes: Negotiating Agreement Without Giving In,* by Roger Fisher and William Ury, the best-seller that provides a short, easy overview of the win/win method the authors call "principled negotiation," and *Win-Win Negotiating: Turning Conflict into Agreement* by Fred E. Jandt and Paul Gillette, which puts a little more emphasis on busi-ness. A day or two with these books should convince any-one that it is possible to negotiate on a win/win basis with the boss, your mate, or even the phone company.

Here are a few specific suggestions:

Don't underestimate the power of your continuing to set a win/win example. Treat your opponent's position as a serious attempt to settle the problem, but an attempt that is just one option among many possible options.

Consider walking away as one of *your* options, particu-larly if the other side is attacking you personally, misrep-resenting facts, or threatening you.

Always consider what your options would be if you *did* walk away. In negotiator's jargon this means considering your Best Alternative to a Negotiated Agreement (BANTA). What, for example, are your possibilities if you don't get the raise you have asked for? What will you do if you can't get the price you want for the house you want to buy—or if you can't sell your house for the price you want?

A well-researched BANTA is actually your greatest source of power in a negotiating situation. It is not, by the way, the same as a bottom line. A bottom line—the price below which you will not go, no matter what—may be useful in certain situations, but it tends to lock you into a certain position. You can only have one bottom line, but the more BANTAs you have, the more power you have. You might even find that one (or more) of your BANTAs is a better option than winning the negotiation. BANTAs lead to more and better options; bottom lines lead to take-it-or-leave-it battles.

Is It Worth It?

Finally, consider whether giving in or getting what you want is worth the cost of a broken relationship. Countless friendships and romances and marriages and family ties—as well as profitable business relationships—have been irretrievably broken over disagreements on matters of "principle" which, in retrospect, seem trivial. As the authors of *Getting to Yes* point out: "In fact, with many long-term clients, business partners, family members, fellow professionals, government officials, or foreign nations, the ongoing relationship is far more important than the outcome of any particular negotiation."

Or, as Fred E. Jandt puts it, "The relationship is much more important than the conflict."

This viewpoint assumes, of course, that there *is* an ongoing relationship—which, as we have seen, is one of the fundamental conditions for creating a win/win situation.

10

Working the Win/Win Way

WORKING FOR YOURSELF is working the win/win way.

Working for yourself is possible, as we will see, in several different situations. It is possible when you work for a publicly-owned corporation, it is possible working in a business you own, and it is possible when you are self-employed.

The self-employed person wants to break through limits. When you feel you work for someone else, you are limited by that person's or company's way of seeing things.

The win/win way allows you to break through the limits imposed by others—as well as the limits you set for yourself. People breaking through limits by working the win/win way are creating the business world of the future.

The Win/Win Manager

Business and industry today require win/win management. In a recent *Megatrends* newsletter John Naisbitt pinpointed the win/win manager's role: "Industry's challenge: shifting from managers who traditionally (and supposedly) had all the answers and told everybody what to do, to managers who act as facilitators, as developers of human potential. For the reinvented, information-age corporation of 1985 and beyond, the challenge is retraining managers, not retraining workers."

If you are a win/win manager, you know that you work for the people who work for you. You are concerned with the personal growth of each employee. You know this attitude profits both you and your company.

Your job as a win/win manager is to allow your employees to win. When they are winning in their jobs, you are, too. Jim Young, a vice-president of Van Schaack Realty in Denver, puts it this way: "A manager derives his sense of well-being from seeing others do well." When the employees win, the organization wins—and you win, too.

The Stick and the Carrot

Stick-and-carrot management—by punishment and reward—does not create a win/win environment. On the contrary, it creates failure, stress, and a lose/win or lose/lose environment.

First, the stick. The most common management errors probably begin with the idea that employees can be controlled through manipulation. Yet the only person we can control is ourself—and even our ability to do that is often questionable. Any idea that involves controlling another person—no matter how clever or well-meaning the manipulation—will lead to failure. The win/win manager sets employees up to win by giving them clear job descriptions, so they know what is required for them to win. There is no manipulation.

Management "by the stick" (by manipulation or fear) poisons the atmosphere of the workplace. To be a win/win manager you must create an atmosphere that will attract win/win people and develop win/win employees. And win/win people will not work where there is motivation by fear. Fear destroys relationships. It also requires the use of more and more fear to produce the desired results. The most common result of manipulative management is employee resentment and sabotage—most of which is never reported, though it costs billions each year.

What about the carrot? Reward—the carrot—doesn't work much better. It's an ever-escalating spiral which demands that you continually give more and better rewards. Rewards and manipulative acknowledgment create dependency, not productivity.

Using such kinds of reward, acknowledgment, and praise as management tools also sets up competition within an organization. Consider the restaurant manager who set up a program of incentives for his wait staff. The idea was to stimulate them to higher levels of performance. It worked for a while—until it became clear that the same top producers won all the time. This discouraged the other employees, and in fact caused much bitterness about how the contests were won. When the program was stopped, the top producers, now accustomed to working for incentives, actually ended up producing less than they had before the program was introduced.

Whenever you attempt to manipulate an employee, your strategy will backfire. Only when your employees are self-motivated and working from a sense of self-worth can you be truly successful as a manager.

Beyond the Stick and the Carrot

What can replace the stick-and-carrot approach to management? The win/win manager has several effective tools and techniques.

Every employee needs to be worked with differently. The win/win manager finds the way that works best for each. The most difficult employee a manager has, of course, is probably the one most can be learned from.

Freedom of choice. The win/win manager treats employees

in a way that makes it clear that the employees should work only in jobs they want to work in. If employees are dissatisfied, they have the freedom to resign and work elsewhere. The win/win manager doesn't blame or penalize employees who choose to work elsewhere, whether in a different division within the company or somewhere else entirely. Win/win managers don't penalize departing employees by refusing them letters of recommendation, or sabotage the attempts of unhappy employees to transfer to different divisions.

One very successful manager in a large real-estate company makes it a point to use his personal contacts with managers in other companies to place salespeople who are unhappy in his office. And, of course, the other managers often return the favor by recommending salespeople they feel would be happier working in a company with a different work environment or philosophy.

The win/win manager hires only those who can align with the values of the company, and then supports them in expressing their passion. If you are keeping employees who need to move on, you are harming both your organization and the employees in question, who probably already know that their passion no longer lies in the work they are doing. The win/win manager is able to fire employees when they cannot win in the company they work for.

Non-Resistance. A manager who must always feel in control is quick to judge, slow to listen, and holds on tightly to his idea of what *has* to happen and how things must be. This creates an atmosphere that stifles creativity and productivity.

In managing by non-resistance, the win/win manager sets guidelines and standards, and then lets work continue apace. The win/win manager doesn't resist the natural way in which the employees work best. The win/win manager encourages the flow of each employee's natural style of working, allowing individual excellence to emerge.

An environment of non-resistance is a relaxed environment. Ultimatums, subtle threats, pressure, and recriminations are the by-products of an overly controlled environment. Harmony, calm, cooperation, and enjoyment are the by-products of non-resistant management. So is a high level of productivity.

Detachment. This management technique is very close to non-resistance. It is based on the principle that the more attached you are to results, the less likely it is you'll get the results you were aiming for. Set your goals—and then let passion, time, and team work for you. In other words, it is necessary to get out of the way of the results coming to you.

Managing with detachment doesn't mean being irresponsible or sloppy. It simply means you do the best job you can while keeping your emotions and compulsion to control out of the way, as these interfere with your passion to do the job. If you are using results to prove your self-worth or to prove you are better than others, you are not detached. Detachment requires a strong sense of self-esteem. At the same time, practicing detachment is a good way to help develop true self-esteem.

Team. The win/win manager consistently thinks in terms of team. He or she tends to use the word "we" a lot. Without thinking about it, a win/win manager talks about how "we think . . ." or "we are . . ." or "we feel . . ." or "what we want to do is . . ." and so on. Win/win managers identify with their organizations *and* their fellow managers *and* their employees. They know what Chester L. Karass and William Glasser, M.D., discovered in *Both-Win Management*: "The group can never win if any member of it loses."

A win/win manager doesn't explain his or her role in the company by stating, "I am the person who gets things done." Those who manage the win/win way say instead, "I am a person who works with others to get things done."

They've found they get a lot more done this way than when they "get things done" by themselves. Or, as Outward Bound, the unique out-of-doors management-training course teaches: "It's not just what you do, but what you do with others that counts."

Paul J. Rizzo, IBM's vice-chairman, says, "We're looking at technologies which are going to involve humanity in every dimension. There is no way any one organization all by itself—without cooperating, collaborating, and understanding others—can be successful." He is not just talking about IBM—he is describing the essence of win/win management.

Cooperating. Understanding and collaborating with others begins with the win/win manager, who knows that responsibility for the business ultimately rests within.

As W. Steven Brown writes in *Thirteen Fatal Errors Managers Make: And How to Avoid Them*: "If you look at your organization and don't like the people, don't blame them; the fault lies with you. If you don't like your volume of business, look at yourself, not just at your market. If you don't like your percentage of profit, don't blame inflation; take a hard look at how you are operating."

Freedom of choice, non-resistance, detachment, and team are the ways of a win/win manager. Use these powerful tools, and your work will become your play. And then, paradoxically, your productivity will exceed all expectations.

The Win/Win Salesperson

Everybody who works also sells.

First, you always *represent* your company or business. Whether you have the responsibility for direct selling or not, you are still always selling your company's product or reputation.

Second, you are always selling yourself *within* the company. You sell your skills, your ideas, your worthiness of the next raise or promotion.

And last but not least, many of us actually sell a product or service directly to customers.

Redefining Sales

Sales is usually thought of as simply selling something to someone—or more likely "anyone" who can pay the price. From the win/win point of view, however, sales is giving people the opportunity to purchase goods or service they want and/or need. It is not the art of persuasion, the science of manipulation, or a four-letter word. People don't want to feel persuaded or manipulated. They don't want to feel used by the salesperson. Very simply, they want their needs met.

One of the critical restructurings of society examined by John Naisbitt's *Megatrends* is that we are now "moving in the dual directions of high-tech/high-touch, matching each new technology with a compensatory human response." In today's increasingly high-tech companies, the customer needs high-touch relationships. The salesperson is the one who can provide this.

This means that the "human response"—otherwise known as relationship—is all-important in any sales interaction.

As Joseph Smith, president of the market-research firm of Oxtoby-Smith says, "A salesperson's theme today needs to be, 'Let me help you' rather than 'Let me sell you.'"

Customer-Oriented Selling

For the win/win salesperson:

Customers must be certain they are winning through the purchase.

The salesperson, also, must be certain he or she is winning through the sale.

For this to happen, the win/win salesperson sells only a

product or service he or she believes is worthwhile. This means that you believe in the product and in the company you represent. When you sell in this way, you naturally acquire "product knowledge"—and you naturally radiate a certain charisma and express a genuine enthusiasm for the product.

Of course, you don't have to be crazy about every single item you sell. (We all have our own particular tastes, after all.) But the best salespeople do enjoy the product they sell. You won't like every dress you sell, for example, but you'll be way ahead if you have a genuine love for clothing and style.

Today's customer wants to know how your product is different, not necessarily how it is better. Be able to make critical distinctions. Differences imply matching products to needs. "Better" is, in the long run, just a point of view.

The win/win salesperson uses neither hard sell nor soft sell. You don't have to use either when you understand the customer's needs and value system.

When your product or service can't best meet the customer's needs or values, recommend that they talk to other vendors in the market—and even suggest other appropriate vendors.

That's right, send them to the "competition" when you honestly can't meet their needs. You can be certain they will come to you when their needs and your product match. And when their friends and colleagues want a product like yours, they'll send them right to you.

Why People Buy

In customer-oriented win/win selling, it is necessary to determine what the customer is *really buying*. Too many salespeople concentrate on "product benefit," and never know why the customer bought (or didn't buy!) a particular product.

Most product lines today are very similar (types of portable hair-dryers, brands of carpeting, even the fundamental components of an automobile). People buy what reinforces their personal value systems and personal needs.

One Harvard MBA and management consultant recently bought a word-processing system. He says that he actually bought the "second-best" system because he'd made a commitment to his new wife to spend more time at home—and since the "second-best" word-processor could communicate with his home computer, buying it meant that he would spend more time at home. He says that the salesman never had any idea why he bought the computer he did.

To get a feel for the way personal value systems and needs can influence sales, look at the reasons, the *real* reasons, why you have purchased items. Look for your inner personal and "selfish" reasons.

Learn the value systems of your customers by establishing rapport with them, making it safe for them to tell you their personal needs and feelings. Nobody does that, of course, when somebody is giving them a "hard sell."

Closing

Most salespeople are taught "the ten best ways to close a sale." Yet most great salespeople can't say when or how they close. Closing for them is a natural part of the sales process. If you watch such salespeople in action, you realize that, whether they realize it or not, they are always in "present time" when they close.

This is exactly what the win/win salesperson does consciously—stays in present time. When you do this your sixth sense—intuition—will be available to you, and you will know *how and when to ask for the order.* And you will do it in a natural and completely uncontrived way.

If you are unable to stay in present time, then use whatever closing techniques you know. That's what they're for.

Overcoming Objections

The win/win salesperson does not meet objections by "overcoming" them. To overcome, says the dictionary, means to conquer or make helpless or exhausted. Obviously this is not the win/win way.

Don't try to overcome objections by attack or defense. Either of these tactics puts you in the loser's seat.

Instead of "overcoming," the win/win salesperson *responds* to objections by being centered—and by incorporating the principles of non-resistance and detachment in communicating with the customer.

The Toughest Objection

Believe it or not, the toughest objections from a customer are always your own objections. The toughest objections never have to do with facts—such as whether or not your PC is compatible with the IBM PC. The toughest objections concern such things as time, money, or opinionated positions. For the win/win salesperson, the customer's toughest objection always reflects the salesperson's own doubts and habits.

Jane, who marketed personal-growth seminars, found her toughest objection was time. She was the kind of person who drove in a carpool, ate breakfast, and polished her nails all at the same time. No wonder she wasn't able to help her customers when they said they didn't have enough time.

Another woman sold vacuum cleaners. Her customers often put her off by saying, "We have to go home and think about it." When asked if she ever used that phrase in her own life, she said, "Well, give me some time to think about it."

Another man insisted that the "toughest objection" theory simply couldn't be true because it would mean the objections were *your* issues and not just the customers'. And anyway, his customers' toughest and most common objection was, "It's just not a high-enough priority." He insisted that he didn't say or do this in his life, ever. Then *he* was asked if anyone in his life told him they didn't get enough time from him. And he suddenly understood. As you may have guessed, it was his wife.

When the head of a brokerage firm heard this theory, he said that there was one case in which he would always lose a sale. If the customer said this one certain phrase, he would simply pack up his briefcase and leave—if the customer said, "Perhaps I can buy it for less tomorrow." He left, he said, because he recognized it was also his own objection.

The solution to the toughest objection is to work through the objection in your own mind first. When you do that, it will be simpler for you to respond to your customer's objections.

You can also work through the objections *with* your customers. As you talk with them about these objections, you'll gain insights that will facilitate your own learning. That is a truly win/win solution.

Rejection

Rejection is the biggest problem that salespeople face. Over and over again they hear the word "No." Many courses, books, training seminars, etc., try to teach motivation techniques showing salespeople how to handle rejection. Some even try to show you how to handle rejection positively— for example, by turning it into understanding or permission or energy or enthusiasm.

Because win/win salespeople sell a product that they love, and because selling that product is their passion, they simply go out and seek business where they expect the answer to be "Yes." If the answer is "No," however, that's fine too. They don't need to turn the *no* of rejection into anything else. They just let it be, stay detached from the response, and move on to the next opportunity.

The Win/Win Entrepreneur

Entrepreneurs are, first of all, people who work for themselves, developing a vision through a business or service.

From the win/win point of view, though, *everybody* who works can be an entrepreneur because we all work for ourselves. "No matter what company I've been employed by," one computer engineer says, "I've always worked for myself."

To work for yourself within a large company, start with simple things such as checking your own work and producing only the finest results. Do this for yourself, for your sense of self-worth and self-esteem. If you work this way, the results will be noticed by others.

Learning how to work for yourself within a company also means learning how to promote what you do—just as all good entrepreneurs must promote their products or services. Let your manager know what you are doing. And be sure to give credit to those who helped you in your best efforts.

People who find ways to work for themselves—even while they seem to be working for others—report to themselves and are responsible to themselves *first*. They are also, more often than not, the first to produce optimum quality and excellence within an organization.

People who have found ways to work for themselves are people who do work they care about, work that interests them, work that means something. They are people who are passionate about their work—people who "work their passion," as we discussed in a previous chapter.

Working for yourself in this way creates job security, high performance, and enjoyment. When you work only for others, it is all too easy to suddenly lose your job due to economic cutbacks or corporate takeovers. But when you work for yourself and are in charge of your work, you have *inner* job security. And it will be easier for you to find another position.

The Business Owner/Entrepreneur

Becoming an entrepreneur who employs other people is not for everyone. But if you think you have found a better way to do or make something, and if you have a taste for risk and adventure and excitement, as well as for lots of hard work, then the entrepreneurial way may be just what you've been looking for.

The entrepreneur's success springs from an ability to *find an alternative*. It could be an alternative to health care delivery systems, computing, or publishing. The next step is marketing the alternative.

Successful entrepreneurs usually feel that they cannot express their vision of a better way within a traditional corporate structure and environment.

Successful entrepreneurs value freedom highly. And they find that freedom by setting up their own business and creating rules, procedures, products, and management that work for them.

Successful entrepreneurs are innovators—they see the world in a different way. They also see opportunities where others see problems. "Innovators seem to thrive during recessions," says William H. Starbuck, the ITT professor of creative management at the NYU Graduate School of Business, "because that's precisely when conservative corporate leaders hold most firmly to the unwritten rules of their trades."

One highly successful entrepreneur says that he gets the most excited and energized when things start falling apart. This is because he knows that each major problem brings with it an even better solution.

The Self-Employed Entrepreneur

Becoming an entrepreneurial business owner requires special conditions. In addition to having a new vision, a better way of doing things, you must have business sense and organization, and, usually, enough capital to start a new enterprise.

Clearly this is not a path for everyone.

For many people, self-employment offers many of the advantages of entrepreneurship—without the high risks and heavy responsibilities.

The number of self-employed people is growing. Self-employed people might work by themselves or with one or two other people. They're involved with computers, and with the organization and distribution of information. Or they work on a "contract" basis for large corporations as specialized technicians and scientists. They own their own trucks and rigs and work as independent contractors for shipping and motor freight lines. They're freelance writers, graphic artists, designers, and photographers.

Self-employed people want to be in charge of their own successes and failures. Like entrepreneurs, they want to be free—free to work their passion, to live their passion, and to express their passion.

11

Bringing the Win/Win Way Home

OUR PERSONAL RELATIONSHIPS—particularly our relationships with those closest to us—can provide us with our greatest opportunities to practice and perfect the win/win way. And best of all, it's in our personal relationships that we can experience the fulfillment and joy of living the win/win way.

The basic idea of a win/win relationship is simple: A win/win relationship means that you *both* win *together*. It sounds easy enough. In fact, it sounds almost redundant. After all, why would anybody be in a relationship in which they were not winning?

The truth, as many of us know only too well, is that very few relationships are win/win relationships. In fact, many relationships are win/lose relationships: one partner gets to win either most of the time or all the time, while the other partner gets to lose. Strangely enough, there are even many relationships which are lose/lose relationships—relationships in which *both* partners get to lose.

Why two otherwise seemingly intelligent and grown-up individuals would play a lose/lose game is a fascinating question, but one beyond the scope of this book. In any case, there is no lack of answers to this question. Therapies and relationship books abound. If you think you are playing win/lose or lose/lose games in your relationships, however, Dr. Eric Berne's classic *Games People Play,* which uncovers the hidden psychological "payoff" in many common lose/lose games, is a good place to start to learn more.

The person who is living the win/win way, however, has already understood that life is not a zero-sum game. (A zero-sum game, as you will recall, is a game in which your loss is my gain, or vice versa.) If life is not a zero-sum game, and if many business transactions are not zero-sum games, then it follows that our personal relationships are most *certainly* not zero-sum games.

And yet again, as we have seen, we are so conditioned to perceive everything in win/lose zero-sum terms, that many of us treat our relationships in exactly that way. And, of course, in a win/lose situation, somebody is always going to be unhappy!

Paul Watzlawick, Ph.D., a communications theorist at the Mental Research Institute in Palo Alto, California, identifies the zero-sum game fallacy as one of the key reasons why relationships go awry.

"Why is it so difficult for us to realize that life is a non zero-sum game?" he asks. "That we can *both* win so long as we are not obsessed with the need to defeat the partner so as not to be defeated by him? And why is it totally impossible for the expert zero-sum players among us to imagine that we can live in harmony with that all-embracing partner, life?

"The first partner only needs to insist on playing a zero-sum game on the relationship level," Dr. Watzlawick continues, "and one may rest assured that things will go to hell."

Setting Your Relationship Up to Win

To make sure your relationship is win/win, ask yourself and your partner two simple questions:

1. Do you want the other person to win?
2. Do you want yourself to win?

Remember, healthy self-esteem is necessary for the win/win way to work. Always giving in to the other person, always putting the other person's needs and wants "first," is not the win/win way. You have to win, too.

Who to Play With

The best partner is someone who is willing to play a win/win relationship game. Obviously, it's nice to have an agreement with your partner that you will pursue the win/win way together.

But it is not necessary. It only takes one person to create a win/win environment, an environment in which the other person can begin to see and feel the benefits of the win/win way.

The win/win way is a path, and win/win relationships are an important part of that path. This means that you will change and grow as you progress along the path—and so will other people. If your partner doesn't see the value of the win/win way at first, simply set the example yourself. Don't underestimate the power of the win/win way. Like faith, it can move mountains. Kindness, generosity, patience, and love are all part of the win/win way.

Negotiating for Couples

Most of us think of negotiations as having a place in business or politics, but hardly in our personal relationships. Business executives who use negotiations every day at the office never think of using their negotiation skills when they come home. One reason for this is that negotiations are traditionally conducted according to the win/lose model—a model that many people feel is not right for personal relationships. But win/win negotiating—negotiations in which *both* parties win—is, as we have seen in a previous chapter, a real alternative.

Win/win negotiations can be an important aid in creating a win/win relationship. If both partners are already committed to a win/win relationship, skillful and fair negotiations can do much to clarify priorities and take your relationship on to new levels of growth and satisfaction. And if, on the other hand, one partner is not yet committed to the win/win way, then negotiations can be an even more valuable tool for demonstrating in a very concrete way just *how* it is the win/win way works for the benefit of both partners.

At the very least, negotiations will protect the partner who has been on the losing end of a win/lose relationship—and perhaps make it clear what changes must take place if the relationship is to survive at all.

In *Winning by Negotiation,* Dr. Tessa A. Warschow, a therapist who teaches her clients win/win negotiation techniques, says, "Many of the problems we experience in our dealings with others, many of the emotional binds in which we find ourselves, don't require long-term therapy and the expense of hundreds of hours and thousands of dollars in order to be resolved. They can be dealt with through the simple process of negotiation."

Dr. Warschow suggests approaching negotiations having to do with relationship-related conflicts—such as sex, love, and romance—in the same way win/win negotiators approach business negotiations. "In business," she writes, "when you want something you make an offer. You say, 'This is what I want, and this is what it's worth to me.' In sex, love, and romance, you seldom make an offer. You wait for the other person to make it. This passive approach rarely works.

"When you don't ask for what you want," Dr. Warschow continues, "your partner doesn't know what to give you. When you don't get it, you become hurt, then angry—and even less able to negotiate for what you want than before."

I Win, You Win/You Win, I Win

In the win/win relationship, you have to able to win yourself—but you also have to truly want the other person to win, too.

In order to support your partner in winning, you have to listen carefully to *what winning is* for the other person. It may very likely not be the same as it is for you. "Listening carefully" means getting yourself and your judgments out of the way—so you can hear what the other person is saying.

The win/win relationship has freedom as its guideline. This means that you must be careful not to infringe on the free will and free choice of your partner. When you listen to him, let him find his own solutions. In this way, you allow your partner to develop the power to win in his own life. Your solutions to his problems may be brilliant, but your solutions may also stifle *his* creativity and rob him of the delight of resolving his own issues. Let your partner work out his own problems; encourage him to grow through his own efforts.

In order to support your partner in winning, you must accept him for exactly who and what he is. Remember, you can't change anyone. All too often, we select a person we want to be in a relationship with, and then we try our best to turn him into another person—a person we imagine we would like him to be. It doesn't work. Nobody can change another person. You can only change yourself. And your partner can only change himself.

It isn't possible to have a win/win relationship if you're

always looking for the "perfect" person. In fact, the only perfect person for you is *you*. You are the perfect person to work with on learning how to love, by dissolving your own blocks and barriers to loving. And it is only through our relationships with other people, as imperfect as they may seem, that we can learn to love more completely. The other, imperfect person is always your perfect teacher. When you find perfection in yourself, you will find perfection in the other person.

As couples counselor Susan Campbell says, "It's more important to love what you've got than to get what you want." It is only through loving *what you've got* that you get what you want.

Lasting

Every relationship needs a purpose larger than itself in order to continue to grow and blossom. This larger purpose may be having a family. It may be gaining certain things in terms of material possessions and security or social status. It may be helping other people or working for peace. It may be developing your intellectual or spiritual lives together.

Businesses often put together "mission statements" in order to clarify their purpose and values. When two people are aligned around a common goal, they could be said to share a common "mission statement" about their relationship. Usually this "mission statement" is either unstated or only dimly understood. Conflicts often develop because both partners have different ideas of what the higher purpose of their relationship actually is. Taking the time to write a mission statement together—which could be revised once a year—can be a very helpful exercise in clarifying your deepest reasons for staying together. Often conflict on a "lower" level can be resolved by remembering the highest purpose of your relationship.

Not Lasting

Ending a relationship is always an option. At times, it may even be the best option. If you are caught in a lose/lose relationship, or if you are on the losing end of a win/lose relationship and your partner refuses to acknowledge the problem no matter how patient and loving you have been, it may be better for both you *and* your partner to end the relationship.

It may also happen that a relationship has simply completed itself, and that one or both partners no longer feel a need to stay in the relationship. In order to end the relationship, the partners get angry, blame each other, and walk away feeling self-justified and righteous.

Ending a relationship in a win/win way means acknowledging the end of the relationship in a different way. It means leaving with love in your heart, having honored yourself and your partner for both the good times and the hard times. It means changing the form of the relationship so that you remain friends.

If ending a relationship means obtaining a legal divorce, the win/win couple will strongly consider using a mediator trained in win/win negotiations, instead of resorting to lawyers accustomed to an adversarial win/lose court battle. Mediation involves *both* partners in the divorce process. Particularly when children are involved, mediation is more likely to result in a fair and lasting agreement for children and partners alike.

Win/Win Parents

Children learn by example. They model themselves after all of your behavior, not just the parts you would like them to. If you master the win/win way of life, your children will use that as their model for thinking and behaving.

Most of us parent the way we were parented. Think

carefully if your growing up was a win/win experience for you. If it was, or if certain parts of it were, pass that on to your children. If it was not, or if parts of it were not, find the win/win alternative, and pass *that* on to your children.

Life can be seen as a series of learning experiences in which we have the opportunity to create win/win from win/lose. Your children will become independent and responsible people when they can create a win/win solution from any challenge. For then your children will have learned to master their world.

It is important not to use competition to motivate or control children—especially since competition is used so often to teach children that the only way to win in our society is for others to lose.

Alfie Kohn, in his book *No Contest*, gives this advice: "A child's performance should never be compared with that of someone else in order to motivate the child to do better. Affection and approval should not be made contingent on a child's performance. This means being genuinely unconcerned with the results of competitive encounters in which the child is involved, including victories. We should be particularly alert to the subtle and insidious ways in which we encourage our children to tie their feeling of self-worth to winning; so long as we need them to be the best in their class, they will get the message and require the same of themselves. The result, we have seen, is not excellence, but anxiety, hostility, and decline in intrinsic motivation, among other things."

This does not necessarily mean keeping children from sports and games that are based on winning and losing. But it does mean teaching them that it is the enjoyment and delight of the game that matters, not who wins or loses.

It also means offering alternative games and sports. There are many sports that aren't based upon competition—aikido, hiking, mountain climbing and camping, horseback riding, and sailing are all examples of recreational activities that don't depend upon winning and losing. Many other examples of noncompetitive games may be found in *The Cooperative Sports and Games Book* by Terry Orlick.

What Your Children Need to Know to Succeed

Most parents are naturally concerned that their children learn how to succeed in a win/lose world, and they try to teach their children how to be competitive.

Win/win parents believe, however, that their children will live in a world in which the old win/lose ways are no longer enough. Here are some of the skills win/win parents might teach their children:

The ability to *cooperate*. This skill will be in higher and higher demand in the future.

The ability to *live in the present*. Children do this quite naturally, of course, but they are hardly ever encouraged to retain and develop this priceless ability.

The ability to *move out of the either/or box of thinking*. The old ways of thinking are becoming less and less effective. People who can come up with new alternatives will be increasingly in demand.

The ability to *discern the difference* between what others say is true and what is true for them.

The ability to *enjoy playing the game* apart from winning or losing.

The Most Important Gifts You Can Give Your Children

Your present time. Your attention and focus.

Showing them how you think through problems rather than acting as if you have all the answers.

A way to contribute to the household and the successful functioning of the family.

The opportunity to develop their unique skills and talents so that they can find, and fully and completely express, their innate passion. Deciding what hobbies and activities are best for them, or what careers they should pursue, robs them of the chance to know themselves.

Kindness.

Listening.

Not living your unfulfilled wishes and desires through your children. A classic lose/lose proposition. Both of you will be disappointed.

An understanding that they are totally responsible for their actions, that they must live with the consequences of their actions, and that the most significant person they are accountable to is themselves.

An understanding that a person can create self-mastery. And helping them find the tools and resources to do just that.

Sensitivity.

A sense of the spirit.

High self-esteem *would* be the most important gift you could bestow on your children, if it were yours to give. However, it is not, by its nature. Self-esteem cannot be given. Your children must develop it for themselves— otherwise it would not be *self*-esteem, but esteem by others. You can, however, create a healthy environment for self-esteem to develop in, by letting your children grow at their own pace. And by loving them for who they are.

Things to Watch Out For

Too much television. The win/lose solutions that are presented on television affect children's thinking and value systems. Commercials also encourage the idea that "winning is the only thing."

Ridicule, harsh criticism, and punishment. Rather than punishing them, let them take responsibility for their actions and mistakes.

In a conflict with your children, work with them to find

an alternative solution according to the principles of win/win negotiating.

Don't let your children vie for the status of *the* favorite child.

Don't compete to be the preferred parent, or the "better" parent.

Don't impose your self-limits on your children.

Don't encourage your children to see themselves as victims, or to blame others. This encourages lose/lose thinking. Again, encourage them to take responsibility for themselves and their actions.

Dr. Tessa A. Warschow sums up win/win parents this way: "They aren't perfect parents. They do become angry at times. They do argue. They aren't always right. Which means they're human. But any child raised by win-win negotiators is very lucky. Win-win parents are firm, but also kind. They are acute and reflective listeners, attested to by the thoughtful questions your own statements provoke. They will encourage you to deal innovatively with problems and to try out many options. They will encourage you to work toward your own goal rather than impose goals on you."

12

The Big Thaw and the Vision of a Win/Win World

SPOTTING IMPORTANT TRENDS is a tricky business these days, especially when a society is changing as rapidly as ours is—and in so many different ways. Lately, however, many of us involved in the win/win way have noticed that something very exciting is happening. The win/win way is quietly showing up in surprising places—and it seems to be happening everywhere, in business, both small and big, in law, in education, and in personal relationships of all kinds. The win/win way is even showing up on the evening news in areas such as nuclear disarmament treaties and hostage negotiations.

In fact, we believe that we are at the beginning of a new era—*a win/win era* that holds unprecedented possibilities for peace and prosperity for ever-increasing numbers of people.

Why Now?

The generation that came of age in the sixties, the well-known "baby boom" generation, is very large—one estimate is seventy-five million. In any case, this generation is bigger than either the preceding or following generation. It's larger than the generation of its parents or the generation of its children.

Convention has it that the influence of the baby-boom generation of the sixties peaked when the Vietnam War ended. Since then, it is said, the idealists and activists of the sixties have given up their old beliefs and become interested in material possessions, money, status, and careers—just the sort of things they once protested against.

This view was popularized a few years ago in a movie called *The Big Chill*, which portrayed the idealism and social activism of the sixties generation as having been supplanted by other pursuits. The characters portrayed in *The Big Chill* were materialistic, cynical, and interested more in their own careers than in helping others. More recently, social scientists and other generation-watchers have told us that young people in schools and colleges are totally involved in choosing careers on the basis of monetary rewards and show a disturbing lack of interest in social problems and causes. Finally, the media have lavished attention on the "yuppies"—young urban professionals notorious for their high-tech and designer-conscious materialism.

A recent issue of the *Utne Reader*, a quarterly that offers a reader's digest of "the best of the alternative press," gathered a number of articles about the current state of the sixties generation under the title "Is Idealism Dead?"

In one of these articles, Michael Ventura, a filmwriter and a popular columnist for *L.A. Weekly* wrote an article explaining the characters in *The Big Chill* as people caught in just this sort of either/or thinking.

"It's not that none of them [the Big Chill crowd] have been true to what were no doubt some pretty naive ideas of what to do with their lives," writes Ventura. "It's that none of them found anything, none of them give any evidence of ever considering anything, except naive idealism on the one hand and a no-holds-barred rush for money on the other . . .

"Here are adults stuck in a convenient either/or system that lets them off the hook completely. None of them ever expresses the idea that they have to take responsibility for the world they live in.

"The film," Ventura continues, "is intended to reinforce the idea that there is no middle ground between idealism and a flaunted materialism. *The Big Chill* is intended to make you forget that both stances, idealism and materialism, are childish yearnings for total and instant gratification. They are each the shadow of the other, and neither has anything to do with growing up. To grow up is to be responsible, and responsible does not mean 'successful.' "

The kind of either/or thinking Ventura describes is, as we have seen in an earlier chapter, one of the hallmarks of the win/lose attitude. The characters portrayed in *The Big Chill* are trapped in thinking that they either retain their idealism or they surrender to cynicism. Either they don't care at all about materialism or materialism is all they care about.

The countertrend expressed by the "Big Chill" attitude has some truth to it, but basically it is just that—a countertrend that merely underlines the prevailing strength and importance of a powerful movement. The values of the baby-boomers and sixties generation have not diminished, in fact, but have simply grown up and matured along with that generation. The sixties generation hasn't become completely absorbed by materialism, and has in fact taken these values into the marketplace—both as consumers and producers.

"Growing up," writes Ventura, "means, at least in part, that one of the things you're responsible for is your world, and in one way or another you have to find a way to fulfill that responsibility. The world is an ongoing act of creation, and you are part of that act. . . ."

Another article in the same issue of the *Utne Reader* is a

study by two sociologists, Professors Jack Whalen and Richard Flacks, who studied student activists and their fraternity and sorority contemporaries, and reported their findings in the *Journal of Political and Military Sociology.* "Contrary to the images of disillusionment and co-optation of youth presented in the popular press," they write, "we have found that while 60s veterans may be disillusioned, they also continue to wish for and seek renewed engagement. If they have married, are raising kids and are holding regular jobs—and worrying more than they used to about money, possessions and advancement—it is also likely that they are trying to be socially responsible in their work, anti-authoritarian as parents and feminist in their daily relationships. . . . Our study persuades us that American society may not have heard the last of the 'liberated generation' as activists working for social change, or as a group that has reshaped the meaning of adult development in our culture."

'60s Going on '80s

How have the values of the sixties generation changed and matured?

Many of the sixties generation saw the world in black-and-white terms of "us and them." There were young and old, hip and square, long-hairs and rednecks, pot-smokers and alcohol users, peaceniks and warmongers, good guys and bad guys, and on and on. The original politics of love and peace quickly gave way to a politics of confrontation and violence—which was one of the things that ended the first period of the sixties-generation influence.

During the seventies many activists became disillusioned with the purely confrontational approach. They realized that the world was not simply divided between us and them, good and bad. The central paradigm—or way of looking at the world—of the seventies became the *holistic* model. People began to realize that in order to understand any given problem, it was necessary to look at all the elements that were present, whether or not they seemed mutually exclusive. Simply put, people began to realize that it was necessary to look at both sides of the coin. This realization appeared in science, in medicine, and in many areas of social conflict. Labor and management began to see that they had to work together in order to survive. The science of ecology taught people how the health and survival of different species of plants and animals were closely related and interwoven with the larger environment of clean air and water.

Searching for alternatives to conflict, people began to explore ways of conflict resolution and cooperation. The win/lose way of thinking began to be replaced by the win/win way.

People also realized that they couldn't change society without also changing themselves. They couldn't change the outer world without either first, or simultaneously, working to change their own inner world. People were becoming more sensitive to the importance of their inner lives, and to the importance of self-fulfillment. The baby-boomers of the sixties generation grew up in a time of unparalleled prosperity. They were taught that they could have it all, and believed it. But it quickly became apparent that having it all meant much more than just having material possessions and exciting experiences. Wanting to have it all also meant looking into their inner selves, searching for meaning and peace of mind. Take a walk through a bookstore and you'll find hundreds of books on self-help, pop psychology, self-fulfillment, and success. Though such books have always been around, there's been nothing like the sheer variety and volume available today.

People today want peace of mind *along with* more material possessions and happiness.

Both of these developments led from a win/lose way of thinking to the beginnings of a win/win way of looking at the world and at social change. This win/win attitude was actually present, at least in its seed form, in the earliest days of the sixties movement, but it was too naive. Many people think that the sixties generation has given up on its ideals and vision in the seventies and eighties, but this is not really so. In fact, the win/win attitude of the mature sixties generation in the eighties is in many ways a return to the earliest and best ideals of that generation.

This maturing of the sixties generation—which we call "The Big Thaw"—can be seen in almost every area of American life.

In music, the newest trend is a meditative type of music called "New Age" music. According to a recent article in *Time*, this is one of the fastest-growing areas of contemporary music. New Age music isn't played on the Top 40 radio stations, but can be bought in record stores and book stores, as well as by mail. It is non-frantic and peaceful, and promotes a harmonious and relaxed inward state of mind.

Ecology, considered a radical idea during the 60s, is now commonly accepted by most citizens, who are concerned about clean air and water and the poisoning of the environment.

The American diet is rapidly changing. People are eating in a lighter, more health-conscious way. They're rejecting the additives and preservatives found in many highly processed foods. The funky local health-food store has been replaced by elegant, well-designed, sunlit markets which sell only fresh wholesome foods. And the person who shops in one of the big chain supermarkets can now find a large variety of natural and healthful foods there as well.

The American love affair with high-stress sugar and caffeine is waning. The candy industry acknowledges that even Halloween candy sales are down as consumers favor healthier and safer treats. The demand for decaffeinated coffee is up, and many restaurants now serve it fresh-brewed. Cutting back on coffee, or totally giving it up, has become a new status symbol in some offices.

Healing centers are springing up in major cities and even in small towns across the country. Offering an alternative to traditional health care (with its emphasis on drugs and surgery), these centers educate consumers in ways to become a healthy person. Viewing health in a holistic way, they focus not just on a well body but also on a well mind, and the interactions between the two. They teach techniques such as biofeedback, meditation, progressive relaxation, and guided imagery. They offer recommendations on diet, allergies, and nutrition.

The fitness craze is also a part of this new health consciousness. Jogging, running, aerobics, and exercise-walking have become part of the new American life-style. People are finding that the benefits of building a healthy body include increased mental stamina, peace, and creativity. In Hollywood and among top corporate executives, one of the newest status symbols is to be advised by your own personal nutritionist or exercise trainer.

Another index of the change in America can be seen in the large numbers of people who utilize counseling and therapy as a way to explore their inner worlds, improve their relationships, and remove blocks to self-fulfillment and success. A recent front-page series in the *Wall Street Journal* addressed the high cost of mental health care now paid by business. Government studies show that five million people sought psychiatric care in 1986, up from half a million three decades ago. In 1984, one in five people had worked with a therapist, up from one in eight in 1960.

Even investment banking, usually the most staid and conservative of professions, has felt the warming winds of the Big Thaw. Socially-conscious investing has become increasingly popular with many young investors. Using slogans such as "Invest in your beliefs," mutual funds such as the Calvert Fund or the Haymarket Fund have attracted socially-conscious investors by promising not to invest in companies that pollute the environment or produce arms. And many of these funds do very well, even when compared with funds which care only about the bottom line. The increasing acceptance of socially-conscious investing has led many major corporations, such as IBM and General Motors, to withdraw their investments in South Africa as part of worldwide opposition to apartheid.

The structure of business itself is also changing under the influence of the Big Thaw. This is the age of the entrepreneur. Many people are starting their own businesses, and are working for themselves. Entrepreneurs find that by keeping their businesses small and flexible, they can change and make innovations much more readily than can large corporations. They also like the flexibility and freedom gained by working on their own terms.

The women's movement of the 70s has also contributed to the new America, especially in the area of relationships. Women have traditionally been the ones who are most aware of the *power* of relationships in all areas of life. As women have slowly been moving into positions of leadership in the business world, the value of relationships has become increasingly recognized. Men, as well as women, have come to see the need for a new way of relating to others in both their business and personal lives.

Government and the political system are so far the least affected areas of all. This is because the Big Thaw generation is between the ages of twenty-five and forty-five, and politics is traditionally the preserve of an older generation. The politically-minded members of the 60s generation are just now getting elected to school boards and state legislatures. When they reach their fifties, and begin to reach positions of national influence, the world of politics will change, and change dramatically. The sphere of politics and international relationships traditionally *follows* rather than leads social change.

The Human Potential

During the 1970s, human-potential therapies and training seminars became the "in" thing to do.

People seeking a better way to live paid their hard-won money to attend workshops run by est, Lifespring, Mind Dynamics, Silva Mind Control, and Transcendental Meditation, to mention some of the more popular.

At the same time, hundreds of other workshops and trainings—from the most ordinary to the most esoteric—became available as well. Today you can find workshops on yoga, primal scream therapy, rolfing, inner tennis, relationship building or relationship ending, women's empowerment groups, co-addiction groups, displaced homemaker groups, men's support groups—and hundreds of groups dealing with psychic phenomena in all shapes and forms. These workshops are usually taught in someone's home or in a church basement or community center. They were virtually unavailable twenty years ago, and certainly were hard to find ten years ago.

In addition, there has been a new surge in the popularity of religions, and the search for religious and spiritual experiences. People are returning to the traditional religions of their childhood with new goals and questions, and they are rejuvenating those religions in the process. They are also exploring the nontraditional churches—Science of Mind, Religious Science, and Unity—and they are seeking answers in Eastern religions, in Buddhism, Hinduism, and Taoism, in Sufi dancing, in Zen meditation, and in the various disciplines and forms of yoga.

These groups and their teachings have certainly been controversial at times.But they have also been highly successful. There are more than one million graduates of est today, and usually half the authors on the *New York Times* best-seller list, at any point in time, have taken est training.

The total number of Americans who have taken at least

one of these human potential workshops or who have become affiliated with a nontraditional or non-Western form of religion is in the tens of millions. Though this number may seem insignificant in a population of over two hundred million, its influence is actually far greater than its size might suggest. The demands, values, and influence of this group affect productivity, civil suits, benefit plans, to name just a few, as well as the products and services which they will purchase—including those they may decide *not* to purchase.

In fact, the numbers of people reached and affected by the millions of others who have participated in the phenomenon called "the human-potential movement" is enormous. It includes fellow workers, bosses, employees, family members, relatives, and friends. It also includes people who have read a self-help book or a magazine article with the hope of improving the quality of their lives and relationships, to say nothing of people who have been affected by the advertisements, television commercials, movies, and songs of people with some experience in the human-potential movement. The advertising slogan of the U.S. Army, for example, is "Be all that you can be." It is also, in a very similar form, a variation of a slogan, "You create your own reality," that many people heard during human-potential seminars years before it appeared on network television. Another example is the slogan "Master the possibilities," which was used by Werner Erhard of est long before TV viewers began to see the advertisements for—what else?—MasterCard.

The Business Potential

In recent years, the human-potential movement has resurfaced in a surprising place—the corporate boardroom and workplace, where there's been a dramatic increase in training programs, not only in technical areas, but in the "softer" areas as well. Many of these programs are actually knock-offs or watered-down versions of the human-potential trainings of the 70s. The concepts presented in these initial trainings have been repackaged especially for business. These training programs constitute one of the country's biggest growth industries—and it is estimated to grow even larger by the end of the decade. In 1985 American companies spent $8 billion to send eight million employees to professional seminars. This amount is expected to reach $12 billion by 1990.

California Business recently reported that *half* of the five hundred company owners and presidents it surveyed had participated in a "consciousness-raising technique" of some kind. California may still be the "leading edge" for this sort of thing, but the rest of the country is not far behind. Ford Motor Company, Westinghouse, and Calvin Klein are among the companies that have utilized human-potential trainings.

A front-page article, "Spiritual Concepts Drawing a Different Breed of Adherent," in the *New York Times* in the fall of 1986 reflects this growing trend.

The *Times* article documents what it calls "the spreading influence of psychological self-help groups that operate under names such as the Forum [which is run by est], Insight, Actualizations, Silva Mind Control, and Lifespring. These group programs for corporate employees attract millions of dollars a year. Borrowing some concepts from Asian religions, the programs try to transform clients' thought processes and to make them better, more creative people.

"Some who have evaluated the trend," continues the *Times*, "attribute it partly to a loss of confidence in traditional Western ideas and conventional ways of doing things and to a willingness to try out anything new in a search for a replacement."

The *Times* goes on to quote Robert S. Colodzin, retired vice-president of Champion International Corporation, and a business consultant. "Why is business rushing in to look at everything from est to firewalking?" Colodzin asks, and then supplies the answer: "The old ways of business aren't working anymore, and even the most intelligent people feel that something's broke."

The same story also quotes Robert Schwartz, owner of the Tarrytown Conference Center in Westchester County, New York, a focal point of innovative approaches to business. "We can see the standard world is not working too well," says Schwartz, "but, in fact, any attempt to explore visions of what the human being might be are regarded as 'off the wall.'

"But it is inevitable," Schwartz told the *Times*, "that people should ask the question 'What is the latent potential of each individual?' We ask this question of iron ores; we are starting to ask it of people."

Employee Potential

Many people, of course, have started to ask the question of themselves, or have been exploring it since the sixties. And many of these people work in American corporations and businesses.

These people—workers or employees or, in some cases, shareholders in businesses—often confuse and puzzle their bosses. They are no longer loyal to the corporation, and they no longer think of it as the paternalistic institution that their fathers once did. They may work for companies, but they are not "company men." In the old days, employees would move anywhere the front office decided they were needed. Now employees think twice, or thrice—and often refuse to relocate because they don't want to uproot their families, or because they prefer the quality of life where they live. And if they do move, they might ask that the company find a job for their spouse.

These employees are not easily motivated, and they often do not respond to the common management philosophies and techniques that worked even ten years ago. They enjoy having things, but acquiring wealth is not their predominant motivating factor. They are, in fact, seeking a better way, a personal meaning in their lives. They want to express their unique skills, talents, and interests in a way that will make a contribution to others, and ultimately make the world a better place to live.

If it sometimes seems that the old ways of doing business are stronger than ever, that is because we are seeing the last brilliant stand of that way of life. Social scientists call this the "sunset" effect. But it makes no difference. The probability of finding a better way has been awakened in too many people. The seeds of change that were sown in the 60s have begun to bear fruit. Business is being transformed both by the people who work inside companies and the people who support those companies as consumers. If the world is not destroyed in a final win/lose cataclysm, and if enough people continue to do their share to make the world a better place to live in both their homes and their businesses, we just may be lucky enough to find that the light of the sunset has changed to the light of dawn— the beginning of the win/win era.

Vision of a Win/Win World

Living the win/win way isn't easy in today's world. In fact, it can be downright tough. At times it will no doubt seem idealistic, stupid, impossible, ridiculous, hopeless. And yet, once you have experienced the win/win way in action— even in the smallest, most insignificant situation—you will find that there is no turning back. The win/win way makes *sense*. It's as simple as that. It makes sense for individuals, it makes sense for families, and it makes sense for businesses. It also makes sense for groups in conflict, for nations at odds, and for the world at large.

It's estimated that at any given point in time there are approximately thirty-nine wars raging on our planet—wars in which soldiers and civilians die very real and bloody deaths. It's also estimated that there are now over five billion people on the planet. Which means that there are five billion internal wars raging as well. These wars within the human mind and heart create their own kind of fear and confusion—a fear and confusion that is reflected in the terrible violence that seems to have no end.

And yet, at the same time, there is an unprecedented movement toward world cooperation, and the win/win way is a part of that movement. The attitudes and techniques being developed by the hundreds of thousands of people involved in win/win thinking offer a very real and concrete way to end the violence and war that now threatens the very existence of the human race—as well as most other forms of life.

Paradoxically, the biggest single factor in the movement toward cooperation is also the greatest danger we face. We are talking, of course, of the specter of the bomb, of nuclear devastation. The bomb is the *universal* enemy. It is the enemy for us, and it is the enemy for the Russians and Chinese. The bomb is our shadow, the final product of millenia of win/lose evolutionary battles.

But it is just this shadow that Albert Einstein spoke of when he said, "In the shadow of the atomic bomb it has become even more apparent that men are, indeed, brothers."

Einstein also said that the bomb had changed everything but our way of thinking. More and more people are starting to see that the win/win option is quite possibly the change in thinking, the proper response to the bomb, that Einstein called for.

In the introduction to Albert Gerstein and James Reagan's *Win-Win Approaches to Conflict Resolution,* which focuses mainly upon using win-win negotiations in international conflict, Dr. Bryant Wedge of Washington, D.C., says, "In pursuing win-win strategies, the participants in conflict seek their advantage. What is new is the realization that this can often be gained without the discomfiture of competitors. Solutions that satisfy one's competitor's needs as well as one's own tend to be lasting. . . . The realization that this is often possible is a new way of thinking: perhaps the new way that Albert Einstein called for to cope with the consequences of the unleashing of the atom."

Dr. Gerstein, who teaches American Culture and Human Communication, and James Reagan, a psychotherapist and organizational consultant, are the founders of Conflict Resolution International. They have tested win/win techniques in some of the most intractable conflicts in the world—with Arabs and Israelis, for example—and found that they can work even there.

"There is a need to plan ahead for conflict so that violent forceful solutions are not needed," they write. "Human beings have the capacity to be responsive and resources are available to meet all their needs. It is extremely important to respect the integrity of the individual and the interdependency of all people on this planet. To do this we must take back the power we have given away to the experts and enter into a partnership with people who have certain technical expertise or specialized areas of knowledge. This entails giving up our belief of helplessness and our positions as victims. Win-win is possible when people work together with intention and sincerity."

The realization that all beings are interdependent is hardly new. Nor is the realization that each one of us can be one with the universe. The Chinese Taoist Chuang-Tzu was talking about all of us, at least in potential, when he took brush to ink in the fourth century B.C. to write, "I and all things in the universe are one."

What *is* new is that we human beings now have the power to destroy the earth—or to break through to a new level of unity and peace from which war will seem as outdated as the dinosaurs. The beauty of the win/win way is that each one of us can move this process forward by beginning to

seek win/win solutions wherever we are—within ourselves, in our homes, in our businesses, with our friends
and adversaries.

The recognition of this global unity is the vision of a
win/win world—a world created by living every day in a
win/win way.

As we have said, it won't be easy, but it will be well
worth it. Every time you get discouraged, think of your
discouragement as your next opportunity to create a new
win/win solution. And every time you want to give up and
go back to your old way of solving problems and conflict,
remember that it's too late for that; once you have seen and
experienced a new way of thinking, once you have glimpsed
a new horizon, there is no turning back.

In fact, the win/win way gets easier and easier with practice. It's like learning a new sport or exercise. When you
first begin to play golf, for instance, it seems impossible to
do everything right and to remember everything you need
to remember at every moment. But after several weeks of
practice, you begin to make some of the moves naturally,
and as you continue to practice, you refine your skills and
keep working on new aspects of the game. You also begin
to enjoy yourself. You appreciate the sky and the green
and the other players in all their wonderful individuality.

Playing the win/win game is the same. After a while, you
will begin to think in a new way. You'll see solutions that
you never would have seen before. And you'll notice that
even in the toughest of times, you are enjoying yourself by
playing well.

In the win/win game, as in golf, the score is up to you.
And although you play with others, the *quality* of your game
is up to you, too. *You* choose how well you are going to
play—and if today doesn't go so well, there's always tomorrow. It's your life, and your game, and remember: by
choosing the win/win way, you always get to win.

Questions to Move You from Win/Lose to Win/Win

These are questions to ask yourself when in a win/lose situation. They are intended to help you find the alternative that will create a win/win. There are no "right" answers; your answers are the right ones for you. Keep in mind that it may take some time and persistence to uncover the answers. *Take the time.* The ideal environment in which to answer these questions is to get a note-pad and pen and to sit down in a quiet uninterrupted place for an hour or so.

What do I want? What do I *really* want?
(Visualize how you will feel when the situation is resolved in a win/win way.)

How can I be true to myself?

Would I rather be *right* or *happy*?

What is my investment in the win/lose situation? What are the benefits to me of continuing on this course? Are they the benefits I ultimately want?

What are my feelings about the situation? Are they appropriate feelings for the situation? Are they exaggerated? Are these present-time feelings?

In what areas do I feel *better than* or *less than*? How am I competing?

What can I do right now to get myself into present time? Is there a present-time activity that would help me to get centered and out of any negative-ego talk?

Have I been in a similar situation before? What can I learn from the past situation?

Am I celebrating wins on a daily basis? What are my wins so far in this situation? How can I set myself up to win? Am I being blocked by one of the barriers to setting myself up to win?

What are the facts? What are all the possible and seemingly impossible alternatives? (Now list all of the alternatives not yet thought of.)

Who is my perfect teacher in this situation? How is this my perfect learning opportunity? (Visualize your relationship to the other players when the situation meets a win/win conclusion.)

Am I working and expressing my passion in life?

Am I either attacking or being on the defensive?

What outcome am I attached to? What can I do to create a sense of detachment? What am I resisting about the situation that seems to persist?

The following questions are the intense "look inside" questions that can lead you to a better understanding of yourself.

Why don't I deserve to have a win/win?

What does this win/lose situation keep me from being, doing, having?

What are the reasons I am in a win/lose situation?

What have I done to create this win/lose situation?

What am I avoiding by being in this win/lose situation?

Who am I trying to punish or get back at?

What do I get to feel righteous about by creating win/lose?

Who would I make wrong by creating a win/win?

Who would I make right by creating a win/win?

Whose love am I trying to gain (and why) by creating win/lose?

Whose love am I trying not to gain by creating win/lose?

What do I feel I am not getting enough of in my life?

B

... And Affirmations to Help You Stay There

Below are seven affirmations which you may find helpful in creating a win/win world. You might also want to create your own affirmations.

- I am carrying the vision of a win/win world in my mind and in my heart.

- I know the win/win way is possible *now*.

- I am remembering that win/lose often "looks like just the way it is," yet win/win is how it is, too.

- I am continually thinking of win/win alternatives to the win/lose scenarios I see.

- I am making my life a model for the win/win way.

- You *and* I are winning!

- I live the win/win way.

Bibliography

Axelrod, Robert, *The Evolution of Cooperation*. New York: Basic Books, 1984.

Berne, Eric, M.D., *Games People Play: The Psychology of Human Relationships*. New York: Grove Press, 1964.

Fisher, Roger and William Ury, *Getting to Yes: Negotiating Agreement Without Giving In*. Boston: Houghton Mifflin Co., 1981.

Gerstein, Arnold and James Reagan, *Win-Win Approaches to Conflict Resolution At Home, in Business, Between Groups, and Across Cultures*. Toledo, OH: Gibbs Publishing Co., 1986.

Heider, John, *The Tao of Leadership*. New York: Bantam Books, 1986.

Jandt, Fred E. and Paul Gillette, *Win-Win Negotiating: Turning Conflict into Agreement*. New York: John Wiley & Sons, 1985.

Kanter, Rosabeth, *The Change Masters: Innovation for Productivity in the American Corporation*. New York: Simon & Schuster, 1983.

Karass, Chester L. and William Glasser, M.D. *Both-Win Management: A Practical Approach to Improving Employee Performance*. Philadelphia: Lippencott & Crowell, 1980.

Kohn, Alfie, *No Contest: The Case Against Competition*. Boston: Houghton Mifflin Co., 1986.

Naisbitt, John, *Megatrends: Ten New Directions Transforming Our Lives*. New York: Warner Books, 1984.

Rausch, Erwin, *Win-Win Performance Management Appraisal, A Problem Solving Approach*. New York: John Wiley & Sons, 1985.

Waitley, Denis, *The Double Win*. Old Tuppan, NJ: Fleming H. Revell, 1985.

Warschow, Tessa Albert, *Winning by Negotiating*. New York: McGraw-Hill, 1980.

Watzlawick, Paul, *The Situation Is Hopeless, But Not Serious (The Pursuit of Unhappiness)*. New York: W. W. Norton & Co., 1983.

Whitney, Charlotte, *Win-Win Negotiations for Couples: A Personal Guide to Joint Decision Making*. Gloucester, MA: Para Research, 1985.